Rural Landless Women Labourers

RURAL LANDLESS WOMEN LABOURERS PROBLEMS AND PROSPECTS

A. Balakrishnan

Publications

KALPAZ PUBLICATION

DELHI - 110052

Rural Landless Women Labourers Problems and Prospects

Rs.690

ISBN : 81-7835-315-6

Published in 2005 in India by
Kalpaz Publications,
C-30, Satyawati Nagar,
Delhi-110 052
Email : kalpaz@hotmail.com

Lasertype Setting: *Tact Computer Graphics*, Delhi
Printed at: Mehra Offset press, Delhi

Contents

Acknowledgements

I wish to place on record my deep sense of indebtedness and gratitude to my Research Supervisor, Dr. S. Kesavan, Professor, Department of Applied Research, for his guidance, advice and valuable suggestions to carry out and complete this work.

I am extremely indebted and grateful to Dr. M.A. Sudhir, Professor and Head, Department of Applied Research, Gandhigram Rural Institute, Gandhigram, for his valuable guidance and advice, timely help and suggestions to carry out and complete the present study. But for him the study and thesis would not have been completed.

I am very grateful to the member of my Doctoral Committee, Professor R.Venkatrathiam, Department of Sociology, Madurai Kamaraj University, for his valuable suggestions and continued support in the completion of my thesis.

I am very thankful to the authorities of the Gandhigram Rural Institute for having given me the opportunity to take up the research work.

I place on record my deep sense of gratitude to Dr.S. Ramaswamy, M.A., M.Phil., Ph.D., Reader, Department of Economics, Gandhigram Rural Institute, for his valuable advice and timely help, despite his myriad commitments.

I am very indebted to Mr. S. Shunmugam, Research Officer, Department of Applied Research, Gandhigram Rural Institute, for his kind support, timely help and encouragement throughout the work.

I am thankful to Dr. P. Arumukham, Professor and Head and Dr.N.D. Mani, Reader, Department of Rural Development, Gandhigram Rural Institute, for their support, encouragement and constructive discussions.

I am thankful to Dr. M.A. Jeyaraju, Professor and Head and Dean, Faculty of English and Foreign Languages, Gandhigram Rural Institute, for his help with the language.

I am thankful to Mr. C. Sivapragasam, Selection Grade Lecturer, Department of Applied Research, Gandhigram Rural Institute, for his support and suggestions.

I am much indebted to Mr. S. Devaraj, Research Assistant, Department of Applied Research, Dr. M. Alankara Masilla Mani, Lecturer and Mr. P.Yogananthan, Department of Applied Research, GRI, for their help and encouragement.

I acknowledge the assistance and help of Mr.C.Asokumar, Mr. K .Seenivasan, Ms. K. Pappathi, Research Assistants, Department of Applied Research. I also thank Mr. R. Elango, Mr. P. Gubendran, Research Assistants, Department of Rural Development. Mr.S. Paulraj, Record Clerk, Mr. N. Murugan Junior Assitant, and Mr. S. Murugan, Department of Applied Research, GRI for their help.

It is my duty place on record my thanks to the staff of the G. Ramachandran Library, Gandhigram Rural Institute.

I express my sincere thanks and gratitude to my mother Smt. A. Laxmiammal, my wife Smt. S. Tamilselvi and my children Ms. B. Haritha and Ms. B. Thariga for their support, encouragement and patience during the long period of my study.

A. Balakrishnan

1
Introduction

Women constitute nearly half of the world population, receive two-thirds of the world's income and own less than a hundredth of the world's property. In India, 90 per cent of women are employed in the unorganised sector, without fair wages and occupational amenities. Domestic women labourers get a paltry sum for the unpleasant work they perform. Some of them are exploited economically as well as physically.

With the growth of industrialization and urbanization, landless labourers, in the absence of assured source of employment in rural areas, migrate to urban areas in search of employment. In urban areas, women are generally employed in informal sectors like weaving, handicraft, tailoring, sale of fish and construction activities.

Unorganised women labourers are outside the reach of most laws which seek to protect labourers, security and living conditions. They are exposed to various exploitations and discriminations.

Indian women, constituting nearly half of the total population, play a crucial role in the domestic sphere and also in the rural field, particularly in the agricultural sector. Yet, our traditional attitude is to treat women as second-class citizens. This is so in spite of the fact that women have proved their mettle in every walk of life. Their contribution is not given due credit. According to an ILO estimate, the value of unpaid household work constitutes 25 to 39 per cent of the GNP.

The largest number of working women in India is engaged in farming operations either as cultivators or as agricultural labourers. They take up a wide variety of activities like sowing of seeds, transplanting, weeding, harvesting, preparation of compost and manure pits, application of manures, storage of seeds and food grains. An active farm woman spends eight to nine hours on the farm during the peak agricultural season.

Rural Labour Market

The poor in India are overwhelmingly concentrated in the countryside and engaged in agriculture and non-agricultural occupations. They are mainly labour households, basically comprising wage labourers and self-employed petty cultivators who are half-peasants and half-labourers. They belong to backward, unorganized and deprived sections of the work force. Even though there have been signs of improvement in the levels of living, particularly during the eighties, the rural labour has been largely bypassed by the process of socio-economic development over the last five decades or so.

In the Indian context there have been several studies which have significantly caused knowing the position of rural labour markets. For example, the pioneering village labour market studies of Rudra and Bardhan (1978) and interpretative synthesis of existing research by Binswanger and Rosenzweig (1981), Dreze and Mukherjee (1987), and Walker and Ryan (1990) have contributed to the theorization of the functioning of labour markets in Indian villages. However, the above limitations of the existing theoretical framework for understanding of rural labour markets operate in India with all their ramifications. Several researches have shown that, apart from market, non-market factors have a great deal of regional variation with regard to the stages of their development. Notable instances are Punjab and Haryana, where more than ninety per cent of all rural labour households are now officially classified as landless (Bhalla, 1992).

Since rural labour markets in India are functionally informal in nature the work contracts, predominance of casual work, and a multiplicity of income sources indicate its close relations with the unorganised sector (Walker and Ryan, 1990; Sharma, 1997). Rural labourers are a heterogeneous group. They may be landless labourers, part-time share-croppers or marginal/small farmers dependent on big farmers for credit and other requirements.

Rural labour comprises both agricultural labour and others engaged in non-agricultural manual work in rural areas. According to the 1991 census, out of 314 million total workers constituting 37.46 per cent of the total population, 79.18 per cent are in rural areas. The agricultural workers (cultivators and agricultural labourers) constitute about 58.99 per cent of the total work force; and of the total agricultural workers 40.26 per cent are agricultural labourers. The result of the five decennial censuses since Independence has shown that the percentage of agricultural labourers to total main workers in the country has gone up from 19.72 in 1951 to 26.09 in 1991. The growth rate in the number of agricultural labourers during 1981-91 was 34.41 per cent (as against 19.65 per cent for cultivators). In 1991 the proportion of agricultural labourers per hundred cultivators was 67 as against 60 in 1981. Females constituted 38.12 per cent of the total agricultural labourers in 1991 and their growth rate during 1981-91 was higher (36.91 per cent) as compared to that of the male labourers (32.92 per cent).

According to the fifth Rural Labour Enquiry (RLE) report (1987-88) there were about 108 million rural households of which 39.7 per cent were rural labour households (including agricultural labour households which accounted for 30.7 per cent). The successive RLE reports, like the decennial censuses in case of agricultural labourers, have also shown a slow but steady growth both for agricultural and rural labour households. The percentage of rural labour households in total rural households increased from 25.4 in 1963-64 to 39.7 in 1987-88. But the proportion of agricultural labour households to total rural labour households has consistently decreased between 1963-64 (85.7 per cent) and 1987-88 (77.4 per cent). This is largely because of the increase in non-farm sources of employment, particularly during 1983 and 1987-88.

There is strong evidence that the definition of rural labour adopted in the RLE is fairly restrictive as it does not fully capture the heterogeneous social formation scenario prevalent in the rural areas covering a large number of rural poor households who are half-peasants and half-labourers. The National Commission on Rural Labour (NCRL) constituted by the Government of India submitted its report in 1991, held that a large proportion of such direct producers is part of the petty production syndrome and, as such, defined the rural labour in the following terms:

"A person who is living and working in rural area and engaged in agricultural and/or non-agricultural activities requiring physical labour and getting wages or remuneration partially or wholly, in cash or kind or both during the year or such own-account workers like small farmers and artisans who are not usually hiring in labourers but are a part of the petty production in rural areas" (GOI, 1991, p. A-3).

Agricultural Labourer

The First Agricultural Labour Committee (1950-51) defined agricultural labourers as 'those people who are engaged in raising crops on payment of wages'. The Second ALC (1955-57) enlarged the definition of agricultural labourer to include 'those who are engaged in other agricultural occupations like dairy farming, horticulture, raising of livestock, bees, poultry etc'. According to the National Commission on Labour (NCL), 'an agricultural labour is one, who is basically unskilled and unorganized and has little for his livelihood other than personal labour'. Thus persons whose main source of income is wage employment fall in this category. It consists of two sub-categories:

(a) Permanent labour (PL) attached to a cultivating household, and

(b) Casual labour (CL)

Permanent (or) attached labourers (AL) generally work on annual (or) seasonal basis and they work on some sort of contract. Their wages are determined by traditional methods. On the other hand temporary (or) casual labourers are engaged only during peak periods for work. Their employment is temporary and they are paid at the market rate. They are not attached to any landlord.

Types of Agricultural Labour in India

Agricultural labour is economically and socially a backward class including the poor tribes and they may be divided into four types as hereunder:

(a) Landless labourers who are attached to the landlords.

(b) Landless labourers who are personally independent.

(c) Petty farmers with tiny bits of land who devote most of their time to working for others.

(d) Farmers who have economic holding but also have one (or) more of their sons and dependents working for other prosperous farmers.

The first type of labourer are almost slaves and are also known as bonded labourers, who do not normally receive wages in cash, cannot shift from one employer to another, and are forced to work for meager wages. In some cases they are supplied fowls and goats by their masters. The other two groups mentioned above have also to suffer though they are considered quite important.

The agricultural labourers constitute an important section of the rural community and they possess certain distinctive characteristics vis-a-vis the other segments of the population residing in the countryside. It is widely known that agricultural labourers are mainly of two types (a) owning land, (generally small holding) and, (b) landless. Certain common characteristics of both these types of agri-labourers are: (1) They have hardly any access to any productive assets. (2) Their own labour mostly sustains them and the price of their labour is generally subject to market forces of demand and supply. (3) They have no stability of employment or destination. (4) There are different forms of labourers, daily, weekly, contractual, piecemeal, monthly, annual, attached labourers and so on. (5) Unlike the industrial workers or white collar workers, they are totally unorganized, and hence tend to be exploited by their employers. (6) There is near absence of Government legislation for this class except the Minimum Wages Act, which prescribes minimum daily wages for farm labourers. But the Minimum Wages Act for them has remained only on paper. (7) Unlike industrial workers and white collar workers they get no other benefits like provident fund, gratuity, medical allowances, maternity leave and so on.

Growth of Agricultural Labour in India

The causes for growth of agricultural labourers are as follows:

(i) High growth rate of population in the country.

(ii) Growth of indebtedness following low income, transfer of land compelling small owners to become agricultural labourers.

(iii) Subsidiary occupations for existence solely allows to enter unorganised units of employment.

(iv) Growth of absentee landlordism.

(v) Disintegration of village communities.

(vi) The extension of money economy to rural areas in replacement of payments in kind.

(vii) Decline of domestic industries and handicrafts.

(viii) Disintegration of the peasantry.

(ix) A severe agricultural depression in the late twenties.

(x) Other social factors like economic transition led to the emergence of this landless class of agricultural labourers and other coolies in the country.

Causes of Poor Economic Condition of Agricultural Labourers

The following are the important reasons for the low wages and poor economic conditions of agricultural labourers.

(a) Low Social Activity– Most agricultural workers belong to the depressed classes which have been neglected for ages. The low caste and depressed classes have been socially handicapped and they never have courage to assert themselves. They are like dumb-driven cattle.

(b) Unorganized– Agricultural workers are mostly illiterate and ignorant, and live in scattered villages. Hence, they could not be organized into unions. In urban areas workers could generally organize themselves and it was convenient for political parties to take interest in trade union activity. This is difficult in case of farm labour.

(c) Seasonal Employment– The agricultural workers find employment continuously for about 197 days in a year and for the rest of the year they are idle. Apart from underemployment there is also unemployment. In rural areas unemployment and underemployment are two important factors responsible for low income and consequently low economic position of the agricultural workers in India.

(d) Paucity of Non-agricultural Jobs– Paucity of non-agricultural occupations in villages is another important factor for the low wages and poor economic conditions of the farm labourers. For one thing the growing pressure of population is increasingly felt in rural areas and the number of landless agricultural labourers is steadily increasing. The absence of occupations in rural areas and lack of inter-regional mobility have also been responsible for worsening the pressure of population on land.

(e) Rural Indebtedness–Agricultural labour is heavily indebted. Normally the farm labourers borrow from the landowners under whom they work. Since they have no security or guarantee in the form of wealth to offer, they pledge themselves to the money lenders and rich landlords and become bonded labourers in many areas. Naturally they are forced to accept low wages.

Landless Agricultural Labourers

The landless agricultural labourers belong to the disadvantaged sections of Indian rural society constituting about 25 per cent of the total labour force. Indeed, they should be paid special attention to lessen their aggravating employment situation and provided with other social security shields. We find a declining proportion of cultivators and an increasing proportion of agricultural labourers. However, the occupational structure has remained more or less stagnant over the last three decades. The percentage of agricultural work force was 69.51 per cent between 1961 and 1981 with a slight increase at present, i.e., 69.79 per cent.

The existing situation in rural areas is such that transfer of land takes place continuously. The process of land transfer has ousted an increasing proportion of rural households from the land with the passage of time. Thus, land transfer has been cited as the principal reason for landlessness. The factors responsible for landlessness, usually law of inheritance, forceful occupation of land and the sale of land are regarded as principal factors for making a person landless.

According to the 1991 census the percentage of rural work force engaged in agriculture and allied activities contributed about 40 per cent of total net domestic production. Of the total population of 88 crores agricultural labourer is 5 crores. The agricultural labourers in India are not only large in number but also are rapidly growing and lead a life of absolute poverty. They happen to be the most backward and exploited class of the rural economy. Indeed, they form the weakest link in the chain of rural economy and present a problem requiring urgent attention. Without a satisfactory solution to this problem, no real progress can take place in the rural sector.

Problem of Landless Agricultural Labourers

The problem of landless labourers is one of the most serious problems in the rural sector. The condition of the landless labourers in the agricultural sphere is deplorable. The number of agricultural labourers in India is continuously increasing. The Planning Commission has admitted that the problem of these labourers is undoubtedly big and complex and that it has not only an important relation with the village economy but will have a serious consequences on the entire economic and social development in the next 15 to 20 years.

Problems of Labourers in Organised and Unorganised Sectors

An organised labour is a protected labour as it has been able to attain (a) reasonable working hours in good working environment, (b) regular employment, (c) periodic wage revision, (d) statutory benefits, and, (e) some social security measures. It is indeed known as a pressure group and exerts some influence on the state. They are powerful and they participate in the economy with their impressive impact on the autonomy of the national polity.

In general the organised labour is well taken care of and their overall conditions are said to be good enough. All their issues are increasingly covered by social security legislation and above all they enjoy considerably better conditions than others.

In sharp contrast to all this is the position of the unorganised labour. It is not confined to employment on the periphery of the main towns, to particular occupations, or, to certain economic activities. On the other hand, unorganised activities are such a way of doing things that a person can enter it very easily. However, while entering the unorganised sector the conditions of work may be relatively harsh. Many factors actually work against this labour force. The very nature of the work of the unorganised labour, that disperses and atomises the work force, makes it difficult.

The Structure and Composition of the Unorganised Sector

The unorganized workers include people involved in agriculture, and agriculture-related work, forest workers, fisher folk, construction labourers, workers employed in small scale/ ancillary units in the informal sector of industry, domestic workers, anganwadi workers, casual/contract labourers, home-based workers and self-employed workers.

Women labour in the informal sector is an important segment on the labour force. According to an estimate of the National Commission on Self-Employment of Women (NCSEW), 94 per cent of the total female work force operates in the unorganised sector.

They do arduous work as wage earners, piece-rate workers, casual labour and paid family labour. The coverage of labour laws has not benefited these women workers in many areas of wages, working conditions, maternity benefits and social security.

According to the 1981 census, nearly 90 per cent of women work in the unorganized sector, which does not offer fair wages and decent terms of work. Nor is there any opportunity to improve the earning potential. There is no supportive services like creches, fuel and water. In the sphere of farm family labour, women's contribution is immense, but no effort has been made to estimate this.

According to the 1991 census, about 81 per cent of female workers are employed in agriculture as labourers or cultivators, constituting 87 per cent of the women work force in rural areas and 17.5 per cent in urban areas.

The NCSEW has highlighted that the unprotected workers are those who are all outside the purview of the organised sector. Sometimes the unorganised sector is divided into institutionalised unorganised sector (IUS) and non-institutionalised unorganised sector (NIUS). Agriculture, agro-based industries, construction work, small industrial units like beedi making, domestic matches, tailoring, garment units, food processing units and other registered units of small scale business are included in the NIUS. These units are supposed to provide regular employment and minimum wages to its workers but, unfortunately, they fail to effectively implement it. And these issues are not uncommon to the domestic workers, sweepers, scavengers, vendors, hawkers and the self-employed.

The concentration of women workers in these occupations is not due to their choice but there is no other alternative for them. Studies also have covered urban workers of these kinds ignoring rural labourers. However, limited studies have dealt with both rural and urban women and their working conditions. Female agricultural labourers are indeed among the poorest section of Indian society with the lowest wage levels (about three-fourths of the male rate) and highest unemployment. Poverty is pushing a growing number into agricultural wage work who were not previously in the labour force or were self-employed cultivators and artisans. This trend is often referred to as the feminization of the agricultural labour force. Despite their increasing prominence in the agricultural labour force rural women are not being absorbed in many of the jobs outside agriculture that are developing in the rural areas. These avenues of employment often require specific skills from women and their socialisation to seek out and adopt to non-traditional work situations.

Rural Female Labour in India

In rural India, women are still predominantly self employed/family helpers. The proportion of casual employees has been increasing during the last two decades. Casual workers form a much larger proportion of the female work force when compared to their male counterparts. On the contrary, the proportion of regular workers is relatively high among the male work force. However, this trend has been declining in recent years. Self-employed workers of men and women categories have been falling in rural areas in recent years.

Women's contribution to the economy by and large remains valuable though their services are unrecognized. Women account for over half the food produced in the developing world, and even more in Africa; they constitute one-fourth of the developing world's industrial labour force; they carry the main responsibility of child care and household chores; they head one-fourth or more of the families in many developing nations; and they usually fetch water and collect fuelwood. Studies in Nepal and the Philippines show that if the production of women is valued properly, on an average, they contribute one-half of the family's income.

The World Bank, in its Annual Report in 1989 observed that 35 per cent of Indian households below the poverty line are headed by women, and in most cases, are thus dependent exclusively on female income. The poorest families thus depend on women's economic productivity. The stress should therefore be on harnessing the strategic potential of women.

The World Bank Report further states that making women more productive "will not merely reduce their dependency enhance their status and security in the family, unless the circumstances accelerate their real growth in unorganised sectors where women constitute nearly half the labour force, to earn for the daily livelihood of the households below poverty line. Such acceleration would improve male and female child survival and increase family investment in education for their daughters, and reduce fertility and slow population growth".

Nearly 92 per cent of the 317 million workers in the country belong to the unorganized sector. These workers therefore remain unprotected by law. They are the most vulnerable section of the society. These 290 million workers enjoy no job or income security with little bargaining power.

Conditions of Women Workers

In the developing world, women are responsible for 50 per cent of total food production. In Tanzania, women work an average of 2600 hours a year in agriculture, while it is only 1800 hours a year for men. In Africa as a whole, 60 per cent of all agricultural work, 50 per cent of animal husbandry, and 100 per cent of food processing is done by women. Millions of women in the Third World cook and clean, sew and wash, plant and weed, care for the old and bring up the young and their working about 16 hour a day is not uncommon.

The unemployment rates among women are consistently higher than those among men. Statistics show that the status of women during three census (1971, 1981 and 1991) periods has marginally shifted from agriculture workers to unpaid family workers. The share of women in non-household industry improved during these years and relatively better paying jobs became available in the transport, storage and communication sector with a marginal decline in other services. However, it is registered just a reversed census period (1991). Thus women are sliding down to low-paying or unpaid work. The declining trend of women participation in the work force may be due to the following three developments:

(i) The technological and occupational structure of the economy might have undergone a male-biased transformation to such an extent that there has been a smaller expansion of the sectors where women workers have a relative advantage.

(ii) Indian economy has failed to attract many potential women workers into the work force. The growth in work participation is not in tune with growth in investment and output. This has naturally caused the composition of the labour force to be tilted in favour of the males; and,

(iii) Urbanization is found to have dealt a severe blow to the rural household industries where women are normally found in large numbers.

Gender Discrimination

Women experience gender discrimination in labour market due to many reasons. Women have lower accessibility than men to productivity augmentation, opportunities like schooling, required training and experience continuity in career and regional mobility. This is referred to as pre-market determination since low-level education, work experience, training and constrained mobility are not consequences of labour market discrimination but the consequences of the discrimination prior to entering the job market.

Women receive less favourable jobs than men or they will not get any job because of their lower education and experience. If tastes for jobs remain the same and qualifications differences are expected, then employment discrimination can take place. Women get lower wages than men for the same job. This is identified as wage discrimination. It can occur in different forms such as collective agreements which can explicitly discriminate against women by creating sex-specific wage groups with lower pay for women.

In India a plethora of labour legislations have been enacted. Unfortunately they provide advantage to one gender over the other. For instance, despite the enactment of the Equal Remuneration Act 1976, gender discrimination is widely prevalent. The Act also prohibits discrimination in employment and recruitment, yet so many hurdles are created by employers to ban women's entry into certain occupations. The law itself does not cater to the gender differences in promotion and advancement. Besides, women are seen as less committed and less productive.

The presence of vast multitudes of rural women as workers and producers in the rural unorganized sector where earnings are low, employment seasonal and insecure, supportive services woefully inadequate or even non-existent, growth opportunities few and collective organization weak, has brought into sharp focus the failure of the mainstream to alleviate their predicament. While it is true that workers, irrespective of sex, are exploited in the unorganized rural sector, women suffer more.

A further discriminating feature is differential wages. It is now common that women get paid much less than men, often for performing similar work. Their earnings are low because wages are discriminatory and work is seasonal and they are the first to be dislodged when work is scarce. Much of the work that women perform is either not recognized or is subbed as subsistence activity.

Women's Participation in the Labour Force

Women's participation has gradually been increasing in most of the countries for a few decades. Such increase in Asia is, however, less marked than in the industrialized nations and Latin America. Within Asia, while this task has clearly risen in South Korea, Indonesia, the Philippines and Thailand, the Indian case is similar to the development experiences of other countries involving a shift of women workers from the unpaid family worker status to that of employees. But this move is not comparatively successful in the Indian context as these women have already got the less advantageous status of casual employees.

Statistics relating to employment status shows that, between 1972 and 1988, the share of women in self-employment and in regular employment has declined. The share of women in casual employment has increased in rural and urban areas. Female employment in India is getting increasingly casualised. This phenomenon may be due to two reasons. First, the employers recruit women as casual workers in order to minimize the financial commitment. Second, with the increase in the sub-contracting of the production process, the employment in general, and that of women in particular, is being gradually transferred from the organised to the unorganised sector.

The conditions of women workers has worsened because of low literacy, i.e., female illiterates in absolute terms are 197.3 million while the number of male illiterates is 126.7 million. There has been further deterioration in the sex ratio, that is, the number of females per thousand males is 929 whereas it was

0934 in 1980s. The disparity between male and female population has widened from nine million to 31 million during the period 1981 to 1991. The committee constituted (1975) to study the status of women in India has found that another problem that affects women's participation in agriculture is the introduction of modern methods of cultivation, which is resulting in a gradual displacement of women and shrinking of their activities. Also, the new agricultural technology has not eliminated seasonality of work. On the other hand, it has only increased the extent of seasonal fluctuations in female employment.

More productive employment on a durable basis appears to be the only panacea to the pitiable plight of the unorganised women workers who can seek better treatment only through collective action. The opportunities for wage employment are limited. Hence, the problems of women workers in the self-employment sector deserve immediate attention.

Problems of Women Workers in the Unorganised Sector

Unorganised labour accounts for 90 per cent of the total work force. Wage employment constitutes only 14.6 per cent of total employment, most of it, that is 9.4 per cent, to be found in the services sector. Of the non-wage employment, 62 per cent records in agriculture and 10.5 per cent remains with industry (World Bank 1995: 148). The unorganized sector is characterized by lack of stability and durability of employment, low wages, lack of job security, absence of social security, unduly long hours of work, non-payment of overtime wages, no leave, unclean, unhygienic and unsafe working conditions, vulnerability to various occupational diseases, accidents causing serious injury also resulting in death or disablement. There are various categories and sub-categories of unorganised labour irrespective of typology such as bonded labour, contract worker, interstate migrant labour, building and construction workers, brick kiln workers, workers of stone quarries, leather, beedi units, tribal collectors of forest produce, salt workers, agriculture workers, fishermen and women, etc.

The women who are working in informal sector occupations are in no way different from the above working force in terms of low wages, low capital intensiveness, low energy use and technology. The women are involved in producing household materials or home-based produced lack visibility due to over-exploitation of merchant contractors and industrial capitalists in the wake of application, non-application of labour legislation, employment regulation and wage implementation. The involvement of family labour often turns out to be unpaid labour.

The women workers in the unorganized sector also lack essential services like creches and child care centres where children are left for care during working hours. Sexual harassment is very acute in this sector. Even young girls and women in many situations succumb to the desires and lust of contractors and employers due to the lack of organizational power and resistance.

Minimum Wage Legislation in India

Most workers in India work in the informal sector. The minimum wage legislation is the main labour legislation for the workers in this sector. In India, the policy on wage determination has been to fix minimum wages in sweating employments and to promote fair wage agreements in the more organized industries. To facilitate the former the Minimum Wages Act, 1948 was passed. A landmark in the history of labour legislation in India, it recognizes that the role of the market and the law of supply and demand cannot be allowed to determine wages of employees in scheduled employments.

The Act provides for fixation and enforcement of minimum wages in respect of scheduled employments to prevent sweating or exploitation of labour through payment of low wages. Once a minimum wage is fixed according to the provisions of the Minimum Wages Act, it is not open to the employer to plead his inability to pay the said wages to his employees. In other words, once the minimum wage is notified under the Act, the obligation of the employer to pay the said wage is absolute. The government can include any type of employment in the schedule. The minimum wage may be fixed at "time rate, piece rate, guaranteed time rate and overtime rate". It can consist of a basic wage and an allowance linked to the cost of living index and is to be paid in cash, though payment of wages fully or partly in kind may be allowed in certain cases. The government can also fix the number of hours of work, provide for weekly days of rest, payment of remuneration in respect of such days of rest, payment of overtime wages and for work on the day of rest at a rate equal to the overtime rate.

Out of the 286 million main workers in India only 27 million or 9.4 per cent work in the formal sector and 259 million or 90.6 per cent work in the informal labour market. Of the total work force 54 per cent are in self-employment, 15 per cent in regular wage employment and 31 per cent in casual wage employment.

The workers in the informal sector work in different employments, and their share in the total work force also varies from employment to employment. Such workers are: (i) contract labourers, (ii) construction worker, (78 per cent are unorganized workers), (iii) casual labour, (iv) workers in small units like handloom, power-loom, beedi-making, tanneries etc. (75 per cent of the workers in manufacturing are unorganized workers), (v) sweepers and scavengers, (vi) employees in shops, and, (vii) workers in agriculture (about 98 per cent of the workers engaged in agriculture are in unorganized sector). Workers in the informal sector do not represent a homogeneous group. They can be classified into the following distinct categories:

(a) Self-employed workers in non-agricultural occupations
(b) Self-employed workers in agriculture-cultivators
(c) Casual and contract workers working for formal sector
(d) Workers in small manufacturing units and small service units
(e) Workers in tiny small scale units

This relates to wage-employed workers in the informal sector, which employs the majority of the work force. In several parts of the economy there is also a shift of activities from the formal to the informal sector. In India, while the percentage of workers, both in agriculture and manufacturing, has declined, that in the service sector has increased over time.

Minimum Wages Based on Workers' Needs

Unorganized sector workers, constituting 286 million in India, work and live in the most precarious conditions. Often they work at back-breaking labour, such as construction work or agricultural labour, for a wage that does not even fetch them two square meals a day. Forty per cent of these workers are women who earn even less than the male workers in the same employment.

The size of the unorganized sector is rapidly increasing with the liberalization policies. In 1979, the unorganized sector constituted 88 per cent of the work force. Today it is nearly 93 per cent. This increase is due to a number of factors. Firstly, the organized sector work force has been decreasing in size. Secondly, there is considerable displacement from traditional occupations and habitats. This includes displacement of artisans due to lack of access to raw materials or to markets. Thirdly, the liberalization policies of the last few years have resulted in falling real wages as well as take-over of markets by large and multinational industries.

The unorganized sector is characterized by a combination of factors. The most important factor is that the unorganized sector workers are not adequately protected. They do not have employment security, they receive low returns or wages, there is no clear and fixed employer-employee relationship, they do not have access to social security. Of course this does not mean that there are no laws or schemes for them. A few of the labour laws such as the Minimum Wages Act and the Contract Labour Act are meant specifically for them, such as Jawahar Rozgar Yojna, Integrated Rural Development Programme, etc. However, on the ground, when we look at the reality, these schemes have limited impact, and the workers do remain unprotected. Another characteristic of the unorganized sector is that the units in which they work are also minimally regulated.

There is a great deal of debate of what constitutes the minimum wage, and it has been often compared to other concepts such as living wage or fair wage. Unfortunately in recent years there has been a tendency to devalue the minimum wage and bring if closer to the poverty line or pauper wage. The latest attempt in this direction is the formulation of the 'floor level minimum wage' which further minimizes the minimum wage. However, every expert body has defined the minimum wage at the poverty level. Even the National Commission on Rural Labour, in its own study, laid down the following principles:

(a) the minimum wage is not the pauper level or poverty level wage;

(b) the minimum wage must ensure the preservation of the level of efficiency of the worker; and,

(c) it must provide for some basic amenities like health and education of children.

What these principles together indicate is that the minimum wage level is that below which wages should not fall. If they fall below that level, the efficiency of the worker will also fall.

In fact the most comprehensive calculation of the minimum wage was made by the Indian Labour Conference and later modified by the Supreme Court in the *Raptakos and Co* case. These norms are:

- Three consumption units for one wage earner
- Minimum food requirement of 2700 calories per average Indian adult
- Clothing requirement of 72 yards per annum per family
- Rent corresponding to the minimum wage provided for under the government industrial housing scheme

- Fuel, lighting and other miscellaneous items of expenditure to constitute 20 per cent of the total minimum wage.

Minimum wage for unorganized workers based on their needs is an urgently required strategy for poverty removal. The unorganized sector contributes in a large measure towards the growth of the economy and it is time that workers in this sector receive the returns for their work through minimum wage, full employment and social security. Unless this happens the economy will continue to be divided into those who are continually growing richer due to liberalization and those who contribute to their growing rich, but do not receive the fruits. No society can continue on this basis for long. It is, therefore, necessary to end the discrimination and integrate unorganized sector workers into the main economy.

Enforcement of Minimum Wages

The Minimum Wages Act, 1948, provides for legal action against an employer if he does not pay the minimum wage. The apex court has observed that "the employees are entitled to a minimum wage at all times under all circumstances. An employer who cannot pay this minimum wage has no right to engage labour and no justification to run the industry" (Supreme Court, 1992, p. 504). Yet, many workers do not get minimum wages. There are several reasons for the poor implementation of the minimum wages legislation. Employees, for fear of losing their jobs, do not report about payments lower than the minimum wages. Sometimes they are even forced by the employers to certify payment of minimum wages. The extended family labour system is also used to evade payment of minimum wages. Above all, lack of awareness of minimum wage provisions is a major reason for its ineffectiveness. This is particularly true in remote areas and in areas where there is no organization of workers.

Many problems arising from the weak enforcement of minimum wages are cited. The scope and coverage of minimum wage legislation are often too ambitious for the administrative and financial resources available with the enforcement machinery. The number of inspectors are inadequate and their training and experience insufficient to cope with the task of implementation. Lack of transport facilities is a common problem in all field work, particularly in rural areas and towns where no branch of the labour office exists. Penalties are almost never imposed on erring employers. Questions are also raised about the capacity of the enforcement machinery.

The most important explanation for the poor enforcement of the legislation in developing countries is, however, the concern felt by the governments over the fact that strict application may increase unemployment, force enterprises out of business and make workers redundant (Watanable, 1976, p. 437; Glinding, 1995, pp. 1446-47).

The implementation is more effective in areas where workers are unionised or otherwise organized and it becomes ineffective where trade unions are weak.

The Eighth Plan (GOI, 1992), however, expressed a different view and observed that a greater role needs to be played by "workers" organizations, non-government voluntary organizations and organized trade unions in ensuring implementation of minimum wages, instead of enlarging the army of minimum wage inspectors for this purpose" (p. 125). This was also the recommendation of the National Commission on Rural Labour (GOI, 1991, p. 213).

In a developing country like India, the main problem of minimum wage legislation is its poor implementation. There are limitations to the enforcement of minimum wage legislation by a government agency. Enforcement of such legislation is more effective in areas where workers are unionised or otherwise organized. A problem in the informal sector is lack of awareness amongst the workers about the minimum wage rates and their entitlement under different labour laws. This is an area that requires the special attention of policy makers, enforcement machinery and trade unions. There is a difference between rhetoric and practice in the fixation and enforcement of minimum wages. To improve the effectiveness of the legislation, the non-government organizations, panchayati raj institutions and workers' organizations should be involved in creating an awareness of minimum wages and in their enforcement, instead of depending entirely on inspectors.

The Equal Remuneration Act, 1976 (No. 25 of 1976)

An Act to provide for the payment of equal remuneration to men and women workers and for the prevention of discrimination, on the ground of sex against women in the matter of employment and for matters connected therewith or incidental thereto, received the assent of the President on February 11, 1976.

Laws pertaining to labour in general and women labourers in particular aim to protect the interest of the labourers in rural areas. But, at the same time, labour laws relating to women strive to provide a lot of privileges and protection to the women labourers as well as their children. In fact women labourers are guaranteed of supportive services like creche, recreation room, latrines and urinals with facilities for child care. Another set of Acts ensures incentives, maternity benefits, leave facilities, intervals for feeding etc. to women labourers. The third category of labour Acts ensures equal remuneration, gender equality in recruitment and prevention of sexual and other exploitation of women at odd hours. The effective implementation of these Acts rests on the attitude of the employers and the awareness of the women labourers in claiming their rights. Fifty years of experience in independent India shows that the above two are still lacking and hence women labourers are still in a plight of backwardness, discriminatory wage structure and deprived of their rights and privileges. The NGOs and government organizations concerned must give special attention to create awareness among women labourers about the labour laws and their amendments vis-a-vis their interests.

Government Measures Pertaining to Agricultural Labourers

Since Independence the Central as well as the State Governments have taken various measures to improve the economic condition of agricultural labour. They include the passing of legislation to fix minimum wages for agricultural labour, the removal of disabilities, the ceilings on holdings and redistribution of land among the landless labourers etc.

1. Indian Constitution—The Indian Constitution has declared the practice of serfdom an offence. It has abolished agrarian slavery including forced labour by law but it will take some time before it is removed in practice.

2. Minimum Wages Act— The Minimum Wages Act was passed in 1948 according to which every state government is bound to fix minimum wages for agricultural and other labourers to uplift their living standards.

3. Other Legislative Measures— The Zamindari system has been abolished by law in all the states and exploitation associated with the system has been removed. Besides, tenant laws have been passed in most of the states protecting the interest of the tenants and labourers, enabling them to acquire the land they cultivate. Many states have passed legislation fixing ceilings on agricultural holdings. The maximum amount of land which a person can hold has been fixed by law.

4. Organization of Labour Co-operatives— Projects such as construction of road, digging of canals, tanks etc., are meant to provide employment to landless agricultural labourers during off-seasons and also to eliminate the possible exploitation of workers by private contractors.

5. 20-Point Programme— In July 1975 the Government of India introduced the 20-Point Economic Programme which included a number of measures to improve the economic conditions of the community in our villages. The revised 20-Point Programme was launched during the Sixth Plan period with measures like :

(a) Speedy implementation of ceiling legislation and distribution of surplus land among landless labourers and small peasants;

(b) Provision of house sites for landless labourers and conferment of the house, if they have been occupying them for a certain period;

(c) Abolition of bonded labour;

(d) Liquidation of rural indebtedness and moratorium on recovery of debts from landless labourers, artisans and small peasants; and,

(e) Review of the minimum wage legislation for agricultural labour to enhance wages wherever necessary.

Special Programmes for Agricultural Labour

Since Independence the Planning Commission has initiated a number of programmes for the development of agricultural labourers. They are:

1. Establishment of small development agencies for farmers, marginal farmers and agricultural labourers (SFDA, MFAL)
2. Integrated Land Distribution and Drought Prone Area Programme
3. Tribal Area Development Programme
4. Integrated Rural Development Programme (IRDP)
5. Rural Landless Employment Guarantee Programme (RLEGP)
6. National Rural Employment Programme (NREP)
7. Jawahar Rozgar Yojana (JRY).

References

Agarwal. A. N., *Agricultural Problems of India,* New Delhi: Vikas Publication (P) Ltd. 1996, pp. 1-15.

Brahmananda, *Dimensions of Rural Development in India*, New Delhi: Himalaya Publishing House, 1987, pp. 72-187.

Harbans Singh Sidhu, *Agricultural development and rural labour*, New Delhi: Concept Publishing Company, 1991, pp. 102-257.

Immanuel, M, *Women and Development*, Ahmedabad: Karnavati Publications, 1998, pp. 21-98.

Kohli, A., *The State and Poverty in India:The Politics of Reform*, Cambridge: Cambridge University Press, 1987, pp. 18-25.

Laxmi Devi (ed), *Rural Poverty and Unemployment*, New Delhi: Anmol Publication (P) Ltd , 1997, pp. 101-161.

Leela Gulathi, "Agricultural labourers", Joyoce Lebra (ed), in *Women and Work in India - Continuity and change*, New Delhi: Promilla and Company, 1984, pp. 62-75.

Loes Schenk and Sandbersen, *Women and Seasonal Labour Migration*, New Delhi: Sage Publications, 1995, pp. 23-155.

Radhakrishna, R and Alakh., N. Sharma (eds), *Empowering Rural Labour in India*, New Delhi: Institute for Human Development, 1998, pp. 1-52.

Raj Mohini Sethi, *Women in Agriculture*, Jaipur: Rawat Publication, 1991, pp. 1-17.

Saran, A.B. and Sandhwar, A.N., *Problems of women workers in unorganised sectors*, New Delhi: Northern Book Centre, 1990, pp 55-184.

Satya Sundaram, *Rural Development*, New Delhi: Himalaya Publishing House, 1997, pp. 208-217.

Savitha S.Joshi, *Women Workers at the Grossroot Level :A Sociological Study*, New Delhi: Ashish Publishing House, 1995, pp. 1-51.

The New *Encyclopaedia Britanica*, London: William Benton, 1979, pp. 25-26.

Tripathy, S.N., *Unorganised Women Labour in India*, New Delhi: Discovery Publishing House, 1996, pp. 1-123.

Uma Devi, Women As Agricultural Workers, *Women's Development, Problems and Prospects*, New Delhi: APH Publishing House, 1993, pp. 27-43.

Journals

Aditya Nigam, Rethinking the Unorganised Sector, *Social Action*, Vol. 47, April - June, 1997, pp. 125-130.

Giankaur, Female employment and wages in agriculture activities - Evidence from Rural Punjab, *Indian Journal of Agricultural Economics*, July -1994, Vol. XVI, No. 3, pp. 54.

Lyakat Ali, Unorganised Labour and the Legislative Measures for their Welfare, *Social Action*, Vol. 47, April-June, pp. 182.

Martin Patrick, Discrimination, Time Allocation and Migration: A study of Unorganised Women, *The Indian Journal of Labour Economics*, Vol. 41, No. 3 (July-Sep 1996), pp. 555-564.

Mishra, L, Organising the Unorganised Labour: Myth, Reality and Possibility, *The Indian Journal of Labour Economics*, Vol. 41, No. 1. Jan - Mar, 1998, pp. 55 - 66.

Nirmala et.al. Genderwise Minimum wages, Wage differentials and determinants: A micro analysis of Agricultural labourers, *The Indian Journal of Labour Economics*, Vol. 41, No. 2, 1998.

Preet Rustogi, Women Employment in the Unorganised Sector: *Social Action*, Vol. 47, April - June, pp. 167-179.

Renana Jhabvala, Minimum Wages Based on Worker's Needs, *Economic and Political weekly*, March 7,1998, pp 500-503.

Sharma,O.P., Unorganised Labour : Some Major Policy Issues, *Social Action*, Vol. 47, April to June, pp. 157-158.

Subesh K.Das, Fixation and Enforcement of minimum wages, *The Indian Journal of Labour Economics*, Vol. 41, No., Apr-June 1998, pp. 327-338.

Sucha Singh Gill, Migration of labour in India, *The Indian Journal of Labour Economics*, Vol. 41, No.4, Oct to Dec, 1998, pp. 617-624.

Sukhadeo Thorat, Social Security in Unorganised Sector in India:How secure are the Seheduled Castes?, *The Indian Journal of Labour Economics*, Vol.42, No.3, 1999, pp. 454-466.

Reports

GOI (1992), Eight Five Year Plan, (1992-1995), Government of India, *Planning Commission*, New Delhi.

GOI(1987), Encyclopaedia of Social Work, *Ministry of Welfare*, Vol. 3, p. 328.

GOI(1949), Report of the Committee on Fair Wages, Government of India, *Ministry of Labour*, New Delhi.

GOI(1991), Report of the National Commission on Wage Policy, Government of India, *Ministry of Labour*, New Delhi.

Watanable, S.H.(1976), "Minimum Wages in Developing Countries: Myth and Reality", *International Labour Review*, Vol. 113, No. 3, May-June, pp. 343-58.

World Bank (1995), *World Development Report*, Workers in an Integrated World, New York.

2
Review of Related Literature

In the previous chapter the role of women labourers and the problems they face at home and at the workspot have been discussed. In the present chapter, related literature is reviewed.

The survey of related literature is an essential aspect of a research report, since it plays a crucial role, especially in locating the research problem. An attempt has been made to gather pertinent information relating to the present study.

Problems of women labourers in agriculture and allied activities

Vivek Ranjan and Bhattacharya (1982)[1] analysed the various problems faced by landless agricultural labourers in rural India, notably meagre wages, paucity of employment opportunities, lack of welfare facilities and discriminatory treatment meted out to them, both socially and economically. The authors further give a warning of the deteriorating conditions of the landless agricultural labourers. The growth of this class has been due to the transfer of land from the cultivators into the hands of absentee landlords, displacement of village crafts and industries by modern industry and gradual transformation of the old village economy based on barter system into a monetary economy based on contract.

Kaur and Goyal (1974)[2] observed the wages of female agricultural labourers in different agricultural operations, based on a study carried out in two districts of Hariyana State at different levels of rural development, namely Karnal, a developed district and Mahindergath, a less developed district. The analysis of data indicated significant differences in the wages of female and male workers engaged in farm operations.

Even such operations like weeding, which are considered to be better performed by women, are dominated by men who are better paid than women.

Sisodia (1985)[3], in "Role of Farm Women in Agriculture: A Study of Chambal Command Area of Madhya Pradesh in India' revealed the indispensability of participation of women in pre-harvest and post-harvest operations of farm business. After studying their commendable services in these activities in a bench mark socio-economic survey of Chambal Command Area during 1983-1985, he advocated implementation of more employment generation programmes in addition to the ongoing rural development programmes for the benefit of rural women.

The study conducted by Erragattusamy etal. (1989)[4] shows that the duration of employment of female labourers is longer in irrigated areas than in unirrigated areas, for instance, between 210 and 265 days per annum in the villages of West Godavari District as against 130 to 220 days in Khammam District. It is also pointed out that the duration of employment is relatively longer in cases of cultivation by modern methods. Another significant finding of the study is that female agricultural labourers, irrespective of their caste or region, are at a disadvantageous position compared to their male counterparts in terms of wages.

Sutra (Social Upliftment Through Rural Action), an NGO, along with R.M.Sethi (1991)[5], has jointly studied the work participation of women in livestock care, home and farm work, and their status with power in the hilly state of Himachala Pradesh. It is clear from their study "Women in Agriculture" that women toil and sweat in agriculture, animal husbandry and other related units in addition to their household burden but their work is accounted as nothing. The women present in the household are responsible for cattle care, the care of a flock of sheep or hens whose produce is marketed for the subsistent need of the family. Self-cultivation of land is their major source of sustenance and their responsibility lies in household chores too. But in all such situations their work is not considered as major economic acts and their contributions to the production process is ignored. In the case of their status the abundant decision making power in all dimensions lies with men alone rather than with women. Hence, the whole services rendered by women in the study area are treated as non-accountable.

Kanthimathi (1992)[6] conducted a study of the economic and socio-cultural variables associated with the participation of women in the labour force in selected agricultural communities of Mayiladuthurai Block, Thanjavur District, Tamil Nadu State. In the study area 50 per cent of the women labour force was absorbed in agricultural work, around 40 per cent fully in household work and less than 10 per cent in other occupations. About 80 per cent of the agricultural labour families were below the poverty line. The contribution of the women labourers to the family income was significant though 40 per cent of the women labourers remained unemployed during off season. There were differences in wage and working hours between male and female workers, and female workers were paid less wages than men though they had to work for longer hours than the males. Comparatively non-agricultural work was more remunerative for women and 73 per cent of them went for work out of economic compulsion.

The study conducted by Ramesh Sharan and Mariswar Dayal (1993)[7] in the Jharkhand region of Bihar reveals that one acre of paddy cultivation involved 80 human days of work, of which female workers accounted for 65 human days. But the wages were lower for female labourers than for men.

The study conducted by Gian Kuar, (1994)[8] examined the participation of female agricultural labourers in the blocks of Gurdaspur District of Punjab State. The female agricultural labourers revceived only 75 per cent of the rate of remuneration for men doing the same work. The female respondents complained of exploitation by their employers in terms of lower wages and hard nature of work.

The socio-economic profile of farm workers is marked by illiteracy, low caste status, low wage, strain, low skill in improved farming methods, lack of access to income and credit, work uncertainty, problem of malnutrition, indebtedness, poverty etc., as summarised by P.Sumangala (1998)[9] in her study of Nilakottai Block in Dindigul District.

In the study on the socio-economic status of women in sericulture in Veerananpet Village of Warangal District in Andhra Pradesh, V.Shobha et al. (1998)[10] discussed employment pattern among women and hurdles to their survival in the study area. Women of all segments participated in silk-worm rearing, reeling, twisting, weaving and other village-based sericulture work for their livelihood. Their contribution to the annual income was in fact considerable. Agriculture formed only a supplementary employment avenue to facilitate seasonal and farm work. These women had to bear the brunt of the additional burden of animal care, feeding, milking and sale of milk. Men rarely came to the rescue of women in these items of work. But the wages paid for their long hours of work was meagre.

S.Gurusamy (1999)[11] highlights the problems of rural women seeking work-low wages, long working hours, seasonal unemployment and consequent poverty and indebtedness, the peculiar features of the Indian landless community. Their rest interval is very limited. Though they are prepared to work throughout the year and all seasons, the seasonal factors force them to be unemployed for most of the time. The writer also focusses on the failure of government policy measures in respect of wages and working conditions.

Work participation of women has been dealt with by Sadhna Tripathi and Sushama Kaushik (1999)[12] in their study on women in mushroom cultivation. Though 60 to 90 per cent of the work in mushroom cultivation was done by women their effective work participation was not appreciated by their men.

T. Ramala Rayalu and V.Durga Bhavani (1999)[13], in their study on profile of girls working in cotton fields reported that these girls work in cotton fields for 9 hours with an hour-long break for lunch and, at times, up to 11 hours in a day, earning an average of Rs.3000 per annum.

M. Jeyamala (2000)[14] conducted a study among agricultural women labourers in Thondamuthur Block, Coimbatore District, Tamil Nadu State. The findings indicated that the empowerment of rural agricultural labour women was very much limited because of their illiteracy and ignorance. Tradition and customs also placed restrictions on their independent decision making. Further, in some cases, husbands would spend their earnings on liquor and sexual deviance. In this situation very little of the women's earnings could be used for children and family.

Problems of Women Labourers in Construction Work

In an inter-state study of Bihar and West Bengal, A.B.Saran, and A.N.Sandhwar (1990)[15] have described the status of female workers in brick kiln, quarry and mine. These labourers were stratified as migrated workers and local workers. The study highlights the exactions of the contractors or intermediaries or brokers, absence of even minimum amenities like potable water, irregular working hours, low wages and sexual exploitation.

S.N.Tripathy (1996)[16] and N.Lalitha (1999)[17] discuss the bad working conditions of female workers in the construction industry, low wages, bondage to intermediaries and insecurity of female workers.

Chitra Ghosh (1985)[18], in her study, brings out the wage differences between men and women in construction work. It is found that though women carry as much load as men, the contractors pay women at a lower rate only. Worse still the labour contractors get the thumb impression of these illiterate women in the register, often paying them less than the stipulated rate.

Problems of Women Labourers in Handloom Industry

S.Sundari and N.Manimekalai (1989)[19] in their study on problems of women workers in the handloom industry at Vengamedu in Karur Block, Tamil Nadu State, have pointed out that women workers in the handloom industry have problems like low wages, insecurity of job, and, lack of alternative employment due to illiteracy and lack of skill. Poverty and indebtedness are the major problems confronting the women workers in the unorganized sector. Further, they found that the wages were far less than those fixed by the Minimum Wages Act despite longer hours of work. They concluded that government and non-government organisations ought to work to improve socio-economic conditions by providing employment and financial assistance and educational institutions should extend education, because education only can bring about a permanent solution to the problems of these women workers.

The pathetic condition of women in the unorganised sector is highlighted by N.Manimekalai and S.Sundari (1991)[20] in their study on "Female Labour Force in the Unorganised Sector of Mat Industry- Some Evidence", which they carried out in Amoor and Ayyampalayam Villages in Tamil Nadu. These women labourers were forced by poverty and destitution to accept low paid and insecure work in the mat industry.

N.Lalitha (2000)[21] has carried out a study on problems of women in cotton textile industry in Dindigul District. Her study, compared the khadi sector and textile industries with regard to women workers. The study was conducted in the Gandhigram spinning centres located in Athoor Block and textiles industries located in Velvarkottai Village of Vadamadurai Block. Since agricultural wokers have to be under the hot sun these workers preferred non-farm work. In the khadi sector all the women workers belonged to landless households and their monthly income ranged between Rs.750 and Rs.1100. The difficulties faced by the women workers in the khadi sector were poor ventilation, excessive heat, wheezing problem, eye-strain, noise from the machine, poor quality of raw materials, leg pain and low wages. Yet none was willing to quit the job due to the prevailing conditions of severe unemployment and poverty. However, the women spinners are better placed in the khadi industry compared to mill wokers. Moreover in textile mills using sophisticated technology, women workers are unable to get their legitimate share due to the low level of their knowledge and pliant trade unions.

Problems Related to Gender Discrimination

A.M.Singh and A.Desouza (1976)[22] have noted that women are highly discriminated against in every occupation in terms of hiring practices, wages and amenities, especially in unskilled and semi-skilled categories, where wage standards are not clearly established.

S.Velayudha Perumal (1999)[23] pointed out that women employees were increasing, especially in less trained, low-paid, insecure and disadvantageous jobs paving the way for discrimination in employment, wage and gender affairs, working hours and various forms of violence.

A study on degradation of women workers among different stages of grass root level women workers was carried out by Savita S.Joshi (1995)[24]. Women were paid less than men's wages for similar jobs. The health conditions of women workers were not satisfactory because of irregular diet. She concluded that women's social condition continued to be traditional, exploitative and anti-women in nature.

The underprivileged can escape all social evils through women employment as perceived by T.R.Gurumoorthy (1998)[25] in his study on "Women in Labour Force: Problems and Prospects". Citing Engelian and Marxian theories in the process of economic development, he said that gender inequality, concentration of women in work with lower wages, lower weightage to women's domestic work, higher fertility and mortality of women, their illiteracy, ignorance and superstitions were some of the major roadblocks in women's economic development. In the author's view literacy could pave the way for curtailing male chauvinism and gender disparity.

Shantha Hariharan (2000)[26] focussed on the deprivation of women in education, employment and politics. In most of our Indian states except in a few states like Kerala, Tamil Nadu and West Bengal, the work participation of women is only 22 per cent out of which 80 per cent is being absorbed in agricultural and allied sectors. Women worldwide face barriers to their advancement and the majority of them are primary victims of conflict and violence. The male child bias in Indian society has created innumerable problems for women in terms of empowerment. Article 14 of the Constitution confers equal rights while Article 15 prohibits discrimination and Article 16 guarantees equality of opportunity in public life, but all practices are derogatory to the dignity of women, who continue to suffer disabilities and humiliations. In other words, this de jure equality of men and women has not yet been translated into de facto practice of equality of benefits in any sphere. Women's representation in parliament and state legislature is also very poor. Ultimately, the ideology of patriarchy and the accompanying culture of silence has conditioned and browbeaten women to accept their disabilities and the discrimination against them as socially ordained and irrevocable. Unless the prevailing bias towards women in social attitudes undergoes marked change women's rights will receive only lip sympathy purely for political ends and the result will be empowerment without power.

Problems faced by the women labourers in family and workplaces

Jaya Arunachalam (1983)[27] portrayed the pitiable condition of rural working women as labourers in farm activities and non-farm sectors long working hours, hard working conditions, sexual harassment and low wages in general and ill-treatment and rape of dalit women by erring landlords in particular. Their illiteracy, under-employment and unemployment force them into slavery in their patriarichical households.

Insecurity and uncertainty, heavy burden, stagnant wages, long working hours and temporary nature of work were found in the occupational structure of unorganised women working as beedi makers, cotton spinners, tea plantation workers, grain mill producers in "A Case Study of Amravati City: The Income, Wages and Working Conditions of Women Workers in the Unorganised Sector", by S.S.Kaptan (1990)[28]. He has reported that these women may not work after 40 years as they had already lost their physical stamina or working capacity by doing long hours of work.

The research on "Women Workers in the Waste Economy" carried out in Ahamedabad City of Gujarat State by Janette Moritz (1995)[29] in collaboration with the Self-Employed Women's Association (SEWA) focussed on the employment experiences of twenty-five paper pickers in the city. This study also brought out the hardships of women in the form of exploitation, lack of protection and infrastructural support, job insecurity, and absense of organised power for collective bargaining. Eighty-eight per cent of the participants started working between the ages of twelve and fifteen and some as young as at nine years of age in agricultural and factory work, domestic service and waste collection.

Nancy David (1996)[30] considered women labourers as arduous workers and wage earners, piece-rate workers, casual and unpaid family labourers without maternity care and other social security measures and Minimum Wages Act. They have indefinable employer-and-employees relationship and can not escape from sexual harassment and other exploitations due to lack of security in life.

Vandana Chhabra (1998)[31] highlighted the significant role of women in household chores besides farm work and other outside services though their commendable and valuable services were degraded and disregarded by their male partners. Even though they share more than half of the burden of men and assist them in so many ways the prevalent practice of discrimination against 'farm women' has continued in the present social system.

According to L.Raja (1998)[32] the rural landless women, especially in the weaker sections, encounter the problem of unemployment and underemployment, low wages and sexual threat by landlords and contractors. Therefore, the SHGs of these women must be activated and strengthened for generation of self-employment.

Violence against women in home and other informal work units even in this age of space exploration and cyber revolution is worse than it was in medieval societies, according to Radhakrishna Rao (1999)[33]. He categorically states that various types of ill-treatment of women cause more death and disability among them than cancer, malaria and tuberculosis put together.

Atanu Thakur (1999)[34] holds the view that discrimination against women has not lessened through government measures taken for gender empowerment even in the present era. He observes that their low interest in the field of education and training in self development has not enabled them to compete with their male counterparts in the high-skilled formal jobs. On the other hand women's household performance in cooking, child rearing, washing and cleaning and other chores is disregarded by unpayment.

Alka Srivastava (2000)[35] has briefly noted the presence of the major section of women force in the unorganised tasks in agrarian sector, small scale industrial units, and home based small scale work units. Collection of minor forest produce, beedi rolling, handloom weaving, fishing, leather work, poultry extension, mining, construction and plantation work are occupations where worker's or labourer's, position is insecure and other socio-economic problems and violence in the work spot, houses and other avenues become normally unavoidable. The nature of atrocities against women in these areas is both acute and widespread and their work force has seen a significant increase in the harassment. The saddest comment is that sexual harassment is regarded as an "Occupational Hazard". Atrocities on women can not be reported to the police because the police, in turn, may indulge in sexual assault.

Problems Faced by the Women Labourers due to Unorganised Sector

The major work related constraints faced by women, according to P.A.Pathak and P.K.Patnaik (1992)[36], include lack of adequate demand for their labour, inadequate workplaces which are poorly lit and ventilated with negative effect on the health of such workers, harassment in the form of availability of less work, high rate of rejection as well as large cuts from their wages, and sexual harassment.

Satyasundaram (1996)[37] stated that the women formed 25 per cent of the labour force accounting for over half of the food produced in the developing world besides their excellent service in household chores. Yet women have been made the most vulnerable section in the society and they have been treated as working machines rather than human beings.

S.N.Tripathy and P.K.Patnaik (1996)[38] found most of the women labourers in the unorganised sector without fair wages and good living standards and in visible vulnerability. Treated as second class citizens, women workers are putting in more hours of work than men and yet without participation in the decision making process.

The rise of female participation in the unorganised sector is tremendously increasing due to economic compulsion, low employment avenues, increasing cost of living and employers' preference, according to Preet Rustagi (1997)[39].

N.Durairaj and R.Kala Rani (1999)[40] stated that economic activities like agricultural processes, traditional professions, small scale industries, petty trades, domestic work, etc. are exclusively done by unorganised female labourers suffering oppression, exploitation, low wages for long periods of work, and paucity of employment. They observed that provision of minimum wages, employment security, and equal treatment through organisational efforts would alone improve their lot.

N.Lalitha (1999)[41] has carried out a study on women labourers in the unorganized sector. She observed the concentration of such labour force in export oriented food processing, textiles, garments and electronics and other small scale enterprises without economically supportive wages and employment security.

Nirmala Banarjee's (1999)[42] study on Women in the Emerging Labour Market highlights women-issues like low status, insecurity in employment and low wages.

Some Strategies to Solve Women Labour Problems

Job-creating schemes, especially self-employment generating activities for both illiterate and literate women are Stressed as the need of the hour by A.K.Chaudhary (1998)[43] in his article "Rural Women Entrepreneurship in India: Bright Prospects". Stressing the importance of creating a favourable atmosphere for the healthy development of women's entrepreneurship under IRDP programmes like Rashtriya Mahila Kash (RMK), NORAD (Norwegian Agency for International Development), NABARD, DWCRA and TRYSEM he stated that awareness creation about these programmes will certainly empower these underprivileged categories to secure employment on their own in the areas of traditional business like agriculture, milk, fisheries, khadi and handlooms, dairy, piggery, bee-keeping, goatery, petty-shopkeeping, pickle-producing, pappad-making, making sauce and other similar products making etc. They should also be enabled to undertake non-traditional business like electronics, ready-made garments etc. in a collective way. The problem of unemployment in rural as well as semi-urban areas can be solved with these strategies.

"The rural women workers are the most backward, unorganised disadvantaged and deprived section in Indian society. They are poor, depressed and even vulnerable," said M.A.Sudhir (1999)[44] in a seminar on Empowerment of Rural Female Force organised in Gandhigram Rural Institute. He pointed out that poverty, lack of continuity and stability in employment, wage discriminations, diverse and difficult nature of work, unhealthy employer-employee relationship, lack of medical care, security and other amenities are major constraints for development. He was also of the view that effective and dedicated leadership to guide and organise female labour programmes for the betterment of these women was lacking in rural areas. Therefore, he stated that social security measures would be successful only if the state functionaries are effective in all the project phases as in states like West Bengal and Kerala. The programmes of the Union Government should be not only employment-generating but also capabability-enhancing to enable women to take up the advantages of these specific schemes meant for them.

Sukhadeo Thorat (1999)[45] made an attempt to study social atrocities against Scheduled Caste and Scheduled Tribe families in our country. He pointed out that atrocities and discrimination on this downtroden people were comparatively much more than on any other farm labour community.

Studies Conducted Abroad

Employment, poverty and other related problems of rural women were studied by Martha Fetherolf (1979)[46] and she presented her findings in the World Employment Conference held at Geneva in 1976. The study focussed on limited avenues of employment for women, overburdened in their routine life. According to the study, fetching water, firewood collection, sweeping, cooking, child-rearing, production of certain commodities like carpets, beedi, lace or beer at home for market and all other agricultural and non-agricultural operations were the low-paid or unpaid indispensable items of work of these underprivileged groups suffering from hazards of unemployment and migration for employment to city or town and even in foreign countries she advocated policy measures for protecting the interests of such women by providing regular employment without much exploitation.

According to Marilou Palabrica (1986)[47] working women in the Philippines have learnt to work within the confines of culturally approved feminine roles as unpaid workers on the family farm, petty traders, waitresses, nurses and teachers. In white collar positions women were heavily concentrated in low-paying and low-status jobs such as factory operatives in the country's new export processing zones or as domestic servants, and all of these workers have been identified with a number of distinct social problems. Even in the Philippines Civil Services the strength of women supervisors was very small. Thus female work activities were generally viewed as "marginal, dispensable, and seasonal".

The status of unorganised farm women in Australian society has been examined by Margaret Alston (1995)[48]. The study analysed farm women's various services in household activities (cooking, washing, cleaning, sweeping, and, garden keeping), farming, building construction and other trades. She observed that much of the work of the women remained unrecognized and unrecorded as these women were described as helpers to male workers despite their heavy work burden. She concluded that their services in house-building, house-keeping and home-making, book keeping, child-rearing, farm management, family maintenance and other services were termed as uneconomic and invisible because of gender inequality.

K.Spio (1997)[49] described Africa as the "region of female farming par excellence" and yet the role of women in the socio-economic process was regarded as invisible in the past in African society. Lack of constitional and legal guarantees would not permit access to women to property rights leading to gender chauvinism.

Conclusion

The review has covered several studies conducted on various aspects of the problems of women labourers in India and abroad, throwing light on the constraints and roadblocks faced by the women labourers. The painstaking efforts of these scholars have effectively brought home the diverse issues afflicting the working women. However they have not specifically addressed themselves to the landless women workers who are the most vulnerable section of the suffering womanhood who are the worst victims of the inequitable economic order and value system of patriarchical society. The present exercise will study the landless female workers, their living conditions and problems which they face both at home and in their workplace.

References

1. Vivek Ranjan and Bhattacharya. *Landless in India - New Face of Rural India.* Metropolitan Book Co.(P) Ltd., March 1982, pp. 205-210.

2. Satham Kaur and S.K.Goyal, Female Agricultural Labourers, *Indian Journal of Agricultural Economics,* Vol. XVI, No. 3, July-September 1974, pp. 512-513.

3. Sisodia, J.S., Impact of Rural Development on Economic Status of Women- Role of Farm Women in Agriculture: A study of Chambal Command Area of Madhya Pradesh, *Indian Journal of Agricultural Economics,* 1985 pp. 223-230

4. M.Erragattusamy, K.Venkatanarayana and N.Lingamurthy, Socio-economic conditions of female agricultural labourers (A case study), *Kurukshetra,* Vol.XXXVIII, No.10, July 1989, pp. 37-39.

5. Sethi.R.M and Sutra *Women in Agriculture,* Rawat publications, New Delhi, 1991, pp. 44-95.

6. Kanthimathi, A study of the economic and socio-cultural variables associated with the participation of women in labour force in selected agricultural communities of Mayiladuthurai Block, Thanjavur District *(Ph.D. thesis),* Madurai Kamaraj University, 1992.

7. Ramesh Sharan, and Maniswar Dayal, Deprivation of female farm labourers in Jharkhand Region of Bihar, *Social Change,* Vol. 23 No. 4, December, 1993, pp. 95-99.

8. Gian Kuar, Female employment and wages in agriculture activities - Evidence from Rural Punjab, *Indian Journal of Agricultural Economics,* Vol. XVI No. 3, July, 1994, pp. 54.

9. Sumangala, P., Female Farm-workers : A Profile, paper presented in National Seminar on *Empowerment of Rural Female Labour Force,* Gandhigram, 1999.

10. Shobha..V., Vimala Devi and Jyothi, Socio-economic status of women in Sericulture, *Kurukshetra,* June, Vol 46, No. 9, 1998, pp. 46-48.

11. Gurusamy. S, Plight of Agricultural Labour, paper presented in National Seminar on *empowerment of Rural Female Labour Force,* Gandhigram, 1999.

12. Sadhna Tripathi and Sushma Kaushik, Women in mushroom cultivation, *Social Welfare,* Vol. 46, No. 5, August, 1999, pp. 7-8.

13. T.Ramala Rayalu and V.Durga Bhavani, Profile of girls working in cotton fields, *Social Welfare,* Vol. 46, No. 2, May, 1999, pp. 23-27.

14. Jeyamala.M, Women Agricultural workers and Empowerment in Coimbatore, paper presented in National Seminar on *Environment and Empowerment of women* at Bharathidasan University, Tiruchirapalli, 2000.

15. Saran, A.B and Sandhwar. A.N, *Problems of women workers in unorganised sectors,* New Delhi: Northern Book Centre, 1990, pp. 55-184.

16. Tripathy, S.N, Women labour in construction sector: A study in Orissa, *Unorganised Women Labour in India,* New Delhi: Discovery Publishing House, 1996, pp. 105-122.

17. Lalitha. N, Female Labour in Construction Industry - Working conditions and occupational hazards, paper presented in National Seminar on *Empowerment of Rural Female Labour Force,* Gandhigram, 1999.

18. Chitra Ghosh, Construction workers, in Joyce Lebra (ed), *Women and Work in India - Continuity and Change* , New Delhi: Promilla & Co Publishers, 1985, pp. 201- 206.

19. Sundari.S and Manimekalai.N, Problems of women workers in Hand loom industry at Vengamedu, *Khadi Gramodyog,* Vol. XXXV, No. 6, March, 1989, pp. 286-294.

20. Manimekalai, N. and Sundari. S, Female Labour Force in the unorganised sector of Mat Industries. Some evidence - *The Indian Journal of Social Work,* Vol. LII No. 2, April, 1991, pp. 195-202.

21. Lalitha N, Comparison of Women Workers in Textile Industry: Khadi Vs. Power looms, *Social Welfare,* May , 2000, pp.10-15.

22. Singh. A.M and A. Desouza, The position of women in migrant bastis in Delhi, *Mimeograph,* Indian Social Institute, New Delhi, 1976.

23. Velayudha Perumal. S, A profile of Rural Female Labour in India - paper presented in National Seminar on *Empowerment of Rural Female Labour Force,* Gandhigram, 1999.

24. Savitha.S. Joshi, *Women workers at the Grass Root Level - A Sociological Study,* New Delhi: Ashish Publishing House, 1995, pp.1-41.

25. Gurumoorthy, T.R, Women in Labour Force : Problems and Perspects, *Kurukshetra,* Vol:XLVI, no.6. March, 1998, pp. 41-43

26. Shantha Hariharan, Women's Rights - Towards Gender Balance, *Social Welfare,* Vol. 46, No.10, January, 2000, pp. 8-12.

27. Jaya Arunachalam, Working Women's Forum in India: An Experiment - Proceedings of conference on *Women in Rice Farming Systems,* IRRI, Manila, Philippines, September, 1983, pp. 105-115.

28. Kaptan.S.S, A Case study of Amravathi city : The income, wages and working conditions of women workers in the unorganised sector, *Social Welfare,* May, 1990, pp. 29-31.

29. Janette Moritz, Women Workers in the Waste Economy, *Economic and Political Weekly* Vol.17, No.1, April-June, 1995, pp. 19-31.

30. Nancy David. I, Plight of Unorganised Women Workers in Tripathy. S.N. (ed), *Unorganised Women Labour in India*, New Delhi: Discovery Publishing House, 1996, pp. 15-26.

31. Vandana Chhabra, The Invisible Women Workers, *Kurukshetra*, Vol.46, No.9, June, 1998, pp.17.

32. Raja. L, Socio-Economic profile and problems of Female Workers in Sadayampatti village, paper presented in National Seminar on *Empowerment of Rural Female Labour Force*, Gandhigram, 1999.

33. Radhakrishna Rao, When will violence against women end?, *Social Welfare*, vol.46, 9 December, 1999, pp. 35-39.

34. Atanu Thakur, A Postmodernist Enquiry into Women's Work Force Participation, *The Indian Journal of Labour Economics*, Vol. 42, No. 4, 1999, pp. 56-60.

35. Alka Srivastava, Women's Rights Rural Women: Saga of Oppression, *Social Welfare*, Vol. No. January 2000.

36. Pathak.P.A, Self help groups and their linkage with banks, *National Bank News review 7*, 1992.

37. Sathyasundaram. I, Plight of Unorganised Women Workers in Tripathy. S.N (ed), *Unorganised Women Labour in India*, New Delhi: Discovery Publishing House, 1996, pp. 1-14.

38. Tripathy. S.N and Patnaik. P.K, Socio-Economic Profile of Fisher-Women Community of Krushna Prasad Block (Orissa) in *Unorganised Women Labour in India*, New Delhi: Discovery Publishing House, 1996, pp. 123-140.

39. Preet Rustagi, Women Employment in the Unorganised Sector; Some Issues, *Social Action*, vol.47, April-June, 1997, pp. 166-179.

40. Durairaj. N and Kala Rani. R. Empowerment of Women Workers, paper presented in National Seminar on *Empowerment of Rural Female Labour Force*, Gandhigram, 1999.

41. Lalitha. N, Women in the unorganized manufacturing sector in India: A sectoral Analysis, *The Indian Journal of labour Economics*, Vol.42, No.4, 1999, pp. 641-650.

42. Nirmala Banarjee, Women in the Emerging Labour Market, *The Indian Journal of Labour Economics*, Vol.42, No.4, 1999, pp. 543-555.

43. Chaudhary, A.K, Rural Women Entrepreneurship in India: Bright Prospects, *Kurukshetra,* Vol.46, No.9, June, 1998, pp. 8-9.

44. Sudhir. M.A, Empowerment of Rural Female Labour Force an Approach Paper, paper presented in National Seminar on *Empowerment of Rural Female Labour Force,* Gandhigram, 1999.

45. Sukhadeo Thorat, Social Security in Unorganised sectors in India - How secure are the Scheduled Caste?, *The Indian Journal of Labour Economics,* Vol.42, No.3, July-September, 1999, pp. 451 469.

46. Martha Fetherolf, Rural Women Unequal partners in development - *UN Report - 1209,* Geneva, 1979.

47. Marilou Palabrica and Costello Women in Development Perspectives, *Manuscript Report of National Conference*: International Development Research Centre, 1986.

48. Margaret Alston, Women and their work on Australian Farms - *Rural Sociology,* 60(3), 1995, pp. 521-532.

49. Spio.K, The Role of women in the Rural Society, *Journal of Rural Development,* Vol.16 (3), 1997, pp. 497-513.

3
Methodology

This chapter presents the problem under study, the objectives of the study, the methodology and the constraints encountered by the researcher in the course of the study.

Statement of the Problem

Women labour is an important segment of the total work force in India. According to the census of 1991, more than 90 per cent of the working women are engaged as wage labourers in the unorganised sector. Although, Indian society has completed five decades of development planning, very little change can be found in the status of the women workforce in India. Most of the women, when compared with the men, bear the brunt of poverty and they are also very often subjected to different kinds of discrimination and exploitation.

A large chunk of them (Census) are employed in the agricultural sector. They belong mostly to socially backward and economically disadvantaged groups like Scheduled Castes (SC), Scheduled Tribes (ST), and Other Backward Classes (OBC).

Women participate in economically productive activities outside the home. Women have worked along with men in the fields right from the beginning of agriculture. The size of the female population and the female workforce in India indicates the potential strength of women in the human resources of the country. The women workers, particularly the rural landless ones, suffer from social disabilities and are prone to continuous exploitation. Their living conditions are very poor and their earnings are very low and are not be sufficient for their subsistence.

In the light of the above, it is necessary to study the prevailing socio-economic status of landless women workers, their problems in the work environment and problems of equation with their husbands and in-laws in home management. This kind of study will enable the researcher to suggest ways and means to promote the welfare of the rural landless women labourers. Hence this study.

Title of the Study

"Problems of Landless Rural Women Labourers in Dindigul District."

Objectives:

The major objectives of the present study are:

1. to study the present socio-economic status of landless women labourers belonging to the farm sector and non-farm sectors in developed and underdeveloped villages in the study area;
2. to find out the problems faced by them in work environment;
3. to examine the problems faced by them in home management;
4. to understand the level of awareness about the development programmes among the landless women labourers; and,
5. to suggest ways and means to promote the welfare of the landless women labourers.

Scope of the Study

Empowerment of rural women labourers is possible only through creation of awareness among them about their rights and privileges. Empowerment also requires dismantling of the existing structure of power, which has inherent class, caste and gender bias. This calls for a complete understanding of the problems of different categories of women labourers and the various socio-economic and cultural factors associated with their work.

It is an empirical study at the gross root micro level and the study will focus on different types of problems encountered by the women labourers in developed as well as underdeveloped villages.

More specifically the study highlights the following areas:

1. the present socio-economic status of landless women labourers belonging to different categories in developed and underdeveloped villages in the study area;
2. the problems faced by them in work environment;
3. the problems faced by them in home management;
4. the level of awareness about the development programmes among the landless women labourers; and,
5. the views of these workers about ways and means to promote their welfare.

The value of the study is not limited to academic purpose only. It can guide the district, and state level officials in formulating policies and programmes for the welfare of the women labourers. It can be useful to voluntary organisations who are already involved in implementing welfare programmes for women and women labourers, especially the poor landless women labourers. It can help other researchers to take up further research work on empowerment of rural women and women labourers. Above all, though the study is limited to a District, such district level studies combined together can enlighten the policy makers and planners at the state and national levels to formulate suitable programmes for involving rural women in economic development.

The purpose of the study the number of terms and concepts has been used which have been explained below:

Woman Labourer

Generally a woman labourer signifies a woman who does the most slavish and less skilled part of a laborious work, as that of husbandry, masonry etc. The terms 'labour', 'labourer', 'worker', and employee are used practically as synonyms and are interchangeable, meaning wage labourer.

Rural Landless Labourers

In the present study "rural" refers to those persons who are involved in agriculture and allied activities and non-farm activities in the villages. Landless labourers are those who are not in possession of land and who are engaged in and depend upon farming and non-farming activities for wages.

Nature of the Study

An exploratory study of descriptive nature, it is a fact-finding survey. "Descriptive research studies are designed to obtain information concerning the current status of phenomenon. They are directed towards determining the nature of a situation as it exists at the time of the study. The aim is to describe "What exists" with respect to variables or conditions in a situation"[1]. Survey method has been used in this study with the help of a pre-tested interview schedule specially designed for collecting comprehensive information for fulfilling the objectives of the study.

Study Area and Sample Selection

This study has been conducted in six villages of Dindigul District. Which was selected in view of the availability of landless labourers involved in different occupations. Dindigul District has 14 development blocks. Multi-stage purposive sampling method was adopted for selection of the respondents Among the 6 taluks of Dindigul District, Dindigul Taluk was selected, since it has a heterogeneous group of landless labourers engaged in various farming and non-farming activities. Among the four blocks of Dindigul Taluk, Shanarpatty Block was used for the pre-test and the remaining three (Athoor, Reddiyarchatram and Dindigul) blocks were used for the actual study purpose in the second stage. The third stage consisted of selecting the six villages at the rate of two villages per block. In each block two villages, one developed village and one underdeveloped village, were selected.

The developed and the underdeveloped villages, were identified on the basis of irrigation and infrastructural facilities. Thus, a total of six villages—three developed and three underdeveloped villages were selected from three blocks, viz. Athoor, Reddiyarchatram, and Dindigul of Dindigul Taluk of Dindigul District. The details of the villages thus selected for this study are shown in Table 3.1.

Table 3.1. Villages Selected for the Study

S .No.	*Block*	*Developed Village*	*Underdeveloped Village*
1.	Athoor	Athoor	Indirapuram
2.	Reddiyarchatram	S. Vadipatti	Kathiriyankulam
3.	Dindigul	Chatrapatti	Kiriyampatti

As already mentioned, the developed villages (Athoor, S Vadipatti and Chatrapatti) are endowed with better irrigation facilities for agricultural purposes and infrastructure facilities like tarred roads, bus transport and accessibility to school in the village itself.

The other three villages have been named underdeveloped because they have moderate irrigation facilities and infrastructure facilities like tarred road, bus transport and accessibility to school in the village itself. The study respondents were selected at the fourth stage of the study.

With regard to the respondents census method covered all the landless women labourers who were identified with the help of balwadi teachers and mahalir mandrams (women's clubs) in the selected villages. The details of women labourers contacted for this study are given in Table 3.2.

Table 3.2. Respondents

S.No. (1)	Villages (2)	Block (3)	No. of Respondents (4)	Per cent (5)
Developed				
1.	Athoor	Athoor	152	30.4
2.	S.Vadipatti	Reddiyarchatram	90	18.0
3.	Chatrapatti	Dindigul	67	13.4
	Total (A)		**309**	**61.8**
Underdeveloped				
1.	Indirapuram	Athoor	65	13.0
2.	Kathiriyankulam	Reddiyarchatram	63	12.6
3.	Kiriyampatti	Dindigul	63	12.6
	Total (B)		**191**	**38.2**
	Total (A)+(B)		**500**	**100.0**

Source : Computed from the primary data.

Data Base

Relevant and required data for the present study have been collected from primary and secondary sources. The secondary data on district, taluk, blocks and villages were collected from both published and unpublished sources. They were obtained from census books, journals, reports, official records, and discussions with knowledgeable persons. Data were also collected from the District Statistical Office as well as from the official publications like Survey of Labour, International Labour Organisations, Indian Labour Statistics published by Labour Bureau, Government of India, and, the various issues of the Economic Appraisal of the Government of Tamil Nadu.

At the village level, the necessary details were collected from the Village Administrative Officers of the selected villages.

Tools for Data Collection

The required primary data for the present study were collected from the landless women labourers. Since the majority of the landless women labourers were illiterate, it was decided to elicit the requisite information through interview method. For this purpose, a well planned structured interview schedule in mother tongue, Tamil, was prepared in consultation with experts working in this field.

Pre-test

The interview schedule prepared was administered to a sample of 50 women labourers in Shanarpatty Block. This block consists of both agricultural labourers and non-farm labourers. The pre-test helped the researcher to revise and finalise the schedule. This interview schedule contained various items required for this study, including the socio-economic condition of the landless labourer families, employment details, problems with husband and with other family members, especially their in-laws, and their suggestions for solving their problems. A copy of the schedule is attached as appendix 'A'.

Apart from the interview schedule, the researcher also undertook field observation to understand the working conditions of the women labourers and their living conditions and the environment in which they live (as Appendix 'B'). Further the researcher held focussed group discussions with the women labourers in the work spot with the help of Mahalir Mandram members and Balwadi teachers in each village in order to get information relating to their working conditions, wages, facilities available at the work spot, health problems due to their physical work, their level of awareness about the work and their rights and privileges. The format of focussed group discussion is attached in the Appendix 'C'. Thus, interview schedule, field observation and focussed group discussion were used as the techniques for collection of primary data for this study.

Data Analysis

For the purpose of village wise analysing the data, the villages were grouped into developed and underdeveloped on the basis of the criterion followed analysing the data, conventional percentage and simple average methods were used. The data have been presented in tables, diagrams and charts for analysis and discussion.

Period of Study

The field investigation and data collection for this study were carried out during the period from October 1998 to March 1999.

Constraints

The study was confined to six selected villages in a district even though results may be generalised for the whole of Tamil Nadu.

The researcher, during the course of his interview with the respondents, faced a number of constraints. Though the respondents were ready to provide all the necessary information required for the study, they were sometimes reluctant to reveal their relationships with their husbands as well as in-laws because of fear. So, the researcher had to be very careful while probing with questions on these aspects.

For collecting necessary data from the field interview and group discussions were used and there could have been some recall bias in these. When the researcher met the respondents in their work spot in order to analyse their working conditions and the facilities, the respondents found it very difficult to explain in detail all the problems they faced because of fear of loss of employment.

Organisation of the Report

The research report has been presented in six chapters. The introductory chapter discusses the need and significance of the study. The second chapter presents an analytical review of the related studies pertaining to the problems of different categories of women labourers conducted in India and abroad. The third chapter states the problem of the study, the objectives, the methodology, the scope and the constraints of the study. The fourth chapter presents detailed profiles about the area and the profiles of area are classified as district, block and village level. The analysis of data is presented in detail in chapter five. The chapter is divided into four sections: Section I deals with the socio-economic status of their families; the analysis of the problems of women labourers in work environment is undertaken in Section II; Section III deals with the problems faced by the women labourers in home management; the problems related to their level of awareness about labour laws and about the developmental programmes are analysed in the Section IV. The summary, major findings, conclusions and suggestions are given in the fifth and sixth chapter.

Reference

1. Lakshmi Devi (ed.) *Encyclopaedia of Social Research,* New Delhi: Anmol Publications Pvt. Ltd., 1997, p. 380.

4
Study Area Profile

The present chapter presents a detailed profile of the study area, namely Dindigul District. It provides information about the district, the blocks concerned and the actual study villages.

A. Profile of Dindigul District

Location

Dindigul District was bifurcated from the east while Madurai District on 15th September 1985 with Dindigul Town as its headquarters. Recently the district was renamed Dindigul District. This district is situated between 77° 30' E and 78° 20' E and 10° 02' N and 10° 50' N. It is bound by Periyar District on the north, Trichy District on the east, Madurai District in the south and Coimbatore District and Kerala State on the west. It extends over an area of 6,058 square kilometers. It has three revenue divisions and is divided into six taluks. The six taluks are: 1. Dindigul Taluk, 2. Kodaikanal Taluk, 3. Natham Taluk, 4. Nilakottai Taluk, 5. Palani Taluk, and, 6. Vedasandur Taluk. The district is further divided into 14 blocks. The study area come under the Dindigul Taluk, which includes Athoor, Dindigul, Reddiyarchatram, and Shanarpatty Blocks.

Climate

In the plains, semi-arid tropical monsoon type of climate prevails. However, the hilly region records low temperature and fairly heavy rainfall. The North-East monsoon is the main source of water in the district.

Population

The total population of the district is 17,60,601 (1991 census). More than 78 per cent of them live in rural areas. The density of population is 291 per sq.km. Of the total population Scheduled Caste population accounts for over 20 per cent. About 50 per cent of the population are literate and the sex-ratio is 976. The occupational structure of the district shows that 61 per cent are engaged in primary activities, 29 per cent in secondary activities and the rest in the service sector. The highest density of population (more than 1000) is recorded in and around the town panchayats, i.e., Palani, Kodaikanal, Dindigul, Natham, Chinnalapatti, Vedasundur, and Gujiliamparai. The northern part of Dindigul District has low density of population, i.e., less than 250 persons per square kilometre. But most of the villages lie in the category of 250 to 500 persons per square kilometre as found in the eastern part of the district, i.e., Vadamadurai, Shanarpatti, Athoor Blocks and some parts of Dindigul, Battlagundu, Nilakottai and Natham Blocks.

Table 4.1: Total Workers Percentage to Total Population by Sex-1991

S. No.	*Particulars*	*Tamil Nadu*	*Dindigul*
1.	Total Workers	43.31	49.12
	Male	56.39	59.66
	Female	29.89	38.32
2.	Rural (Total)	48.49	53.29
	Male	58.28	61.34
	Female	38.50	45.06
3.	Urban (Total)	33.34	33.82
	Male	52.78	53.54
	Female	13.10	13.43

Source: 1991 census.

The total population of the district, according to the 1991 census, is 17,60,601 persons, comprising 8,90,783 males and 8,69,818 females. The rural population of the district is 13,83,580 persons (6,99,122 males and 6,84,458 females) and the urban population is 3,77,021 persons (1,91,661 males and 1,85,360 females). According to the 1991 census, total literates (excluding the population in the age group of 0-6 years) is 8,73,499 persons. Of these, 5,37,829 are males and 3,35,670 are females. In the rural areas of the district, 6,16,480 persons (3,92,930 males and 2,23,550 females) are literates and in the urban areas 2,57,019 persons (1,44,899 males and 1,12,120 females) are literates.

Land use and Cropping Pattern

The spatial distribution of major land use and land cover includes built-up land, agricultural land, forest, waste land, water bodies, mining areas and grazing land. Built-up lands are found in and around Dindigul, Palani, Kodaikanal, Vedasandur and Natham Towns. Area under forest is found in the south-western and the eastern parts of the district. It is also found in small pockets in the southern and the north-eastern parts of the district. Waste lands are found largely in the south-western and the eastern parts of the district. They are also found in some pockets in the northern part of the district. Grazing lands are found in a few locations in the south-western part of the district. The rest of the area comes under agricultural land.

The total geographical area of the district is 5,08,016 hectares and net cultivable area is 2,74,707 hectares. Out of the net area sown, as low as 9 per cent is sown more than once. Dry farming is predominant in the district and the important wet land tracts are located in the Shanmuganathi and the Kodaganar basins. Paddy is the principal crop (37 per cent), followed by oil seeds (23 per cent) and fruits and vegetables (24 per cent). Sirumalai and Virupatchi Hills are known for a special variety of plantains. Fruits like orange, lime, mango and grape are the specialities of Dindigul, Nilakottai and Palani Taluks. In the plains region, the important crops are paddy, cholam, cumbu, millets, oil seeds, cotton, sugarcane, onion, etc. In the Kodaikanal and the Sirumalai Hills, the major crops are coffee, citrus fruits, etc.

Forests

Dindigul forest division covers the entire district, except Kodaikanal division, and has eight ranges. Both the divisions have reserved forests as well as reserved lands. In Dindigul division, the eastern part, i.e., eastern part of Gujiliamparai and Vadamadurai Blocks, the north-eastern part of Vedasandur Block, Sirumalai Hills and the hilly area of Natham Block, the northern slopes of the Palani Hills have reserved forests. Three pockets of reserved lands are found in the Sirumalai Hills, the eastern Lower Palani Hills and the north- central slope of Palani Hills. In Kodaikanal forest division, reserved forest covers the major area and reserved lands occupy a small area.

Net Area Sown

Net area sown in the district is 58 per cent of the total area. It is observed that the north-western, the central and the south-eastern parts of the district, i.e., Thoppampatti, Palani, Reddiarchatram and Natham Blocks stand out predominantly, with more than 70 per cent of cultivable land. It is less than 40 per cent in the dry blocks, viz., Gujiliamparai and Vedasandur. Kodaikanal Block and the western part of Reddiarchatram Block have smaller area because of hilly terrain. The majority of the villages in the eastern and the central part of the district are in the category with less than 40 per cent of net sown area.

Area Sown More than Once

Most of the area of the district is not sown more than once. The area sown more than once as percentage of net sown area is marginal, i.e., within one to five per cent. Concentration of area sown more than once at ten per cent is found in Vadamadurai and Natham Blocks. Selected villages in Gujiliamparai,

Vadamadurai, Battalagundu, Nilakottai and Athoor Blocks are cultivated more than once.

Physiography and Relief

The district has extensive hilly and rocky areas with undulating plains. Palani Hills, forming the northern spur of the Western Ghats, ranges in height from 1000 to 2700 metres. The Upper Palani Hills, with an average height of 2500 metres, has four important valleys viz., Kudirayar Valley, Porandalar Valley, Pallar Valley and Marudanathi Valley and several peaks like Perumal Hill, Pallangi Hill, Vembadi Shola Peak, etc. The Lower Palani Hills consists of a confused jumble of hills from 1000 to 1200 metres height, separated from one another by steep and beautiful wooded valleys. Those hills are Thandikudi, Virupakshi Hill, etc. On the eastern side, Sirumalai, Alagarmalai, Natham and Ayyalur Hills are found. Many isolated hills viz., Modukamalai, Karandamalai, the Great Rock of Dindigul etc., are also found. The hilly terrain the south-west and east slope down steeply in the northern direction and towards the central part of the district.

Irrigation

In this district the predominant source of irrigation is well. The important irrigation schemes are Palar, Porandalar, Kodaganar and Manjalar. In the plains, dry farming is practised with the exception of Shanmuganadhi and Kodaganar river basins.

Rainfall

The annual rainfall is about 1214.50 mm (excluding Kodaikanal), which is more than double the normal rainfall of the state (normal rainfall 500 mm). As for seasonal distribution, the full benefit of the South-West monsoon could not be harvested because of the Western Ghats forming a barrier. The North-East monsoon is the principal monsoon. The remaining two seasons, namely winter and summer, are insignificant. Floods have occurred occasionally. Dindigul and Vedasandur Taluks are the driest parts.

Industry

Some of the fast developing industrial activities of recent origin are lime-kiln, brick-kiln, spinning and paper mills. Other traditional but important industries are leather tanning, lock making, brassware industry, tobacco and cigar making, jewellery work, dyeing, art silk weaving etc. Next to farming, a sizable population depends on industries. Dindigul is an important industrial centre.

A number of spinning mills are coming up in Vedasandur and Vadamadurai Blocks, besides a few paper mills in Swaminatha-puram. A mini steel industry has been established. Tobacco and cigar, metal, dyes, iron, cotton spinning and weaving are the other promising industries. The district thrives with handloom industry in Chinnalapatti, which is located 11 kilometres away from Dindigul. Chinnalapatti art silk sarees and Sungudi (cotton) sarees are famous throughout India. More than 1,000 families are engaged in the industry. In addition, Khadi industry (spinning, weaving, and dyeing) has been promoted by Gandhigram in a big way. An industrial estate is available at Dindigul for the benefit of small scale industries.

Infrastructure Facilities

Dindigul and Palani are the two important educational centres with arts and science colleges, professional colleges and polytechnics. The district has two universities namely Gandhigram Rural Institute, Gandhigram and Mother Teresa Women's University, Kodaikanal. There are 1351 schools functioning in the district. The district has nine hospitals, 31 primary health centres and 307 sub-centres. Agricultural produce are marketed in six permanent and six regulated markets, along with seven unregulated markets and seven shanties. With regard to veterinary facilities, four hospitals, 27 dispensaries, 11 key village sub-centres and one poultry extension centre are providing services to the livestock population. The district has a good road net-work, well connected with other parts of the State. National Highway No. 7 and 47 run through the district. Surfaced road length is 3071 km while unsurfaced length is 3071.37 km. Metre gauge railway line connects the district with Coimbatore and Madurai while broad gauge links with Karur, Tiruchirappalli, Madurai and Madras.

B. Block and Village Profiles

The study area consists of both developed and underdeveloped category of villages with a sample of two villages each from Athoor, Reddiarchatram and Dindigul Blocks respectively. These blocks are notable ones in Dindigul District. Dindigul is the District headquarters while Athoor Block is the catchment base for the supply of drinking water and Reddiarchatram is the pilgrimage block with a famous temple. Each block is discussed briefly hereunder.

Block Profile

Dindigul Block consists of two town panchayats and six village panchayats. The total population is 95,145 of which males are 48,342 and females 46,803. The Scheduled Caste population is 25,749, of which males are 13,000 and females 12,149. In Dindigul Block, Dindigul Town is the headquarters of the district, the taluk and the block. Dindigul has the highest concentration of population and all the higher level educational institutions are located in the Dindigul Town.

Total geographical area of Dindigul Block is 10916.8 hectares and the land use classification is as shown below:

1. Total Area under cultivation – 4729.98 hectares
2. Net cultivable land – 3779.88 hectares
3. Uncultivable land for other uses – 1739.53 hectares
4. Cultivable waste – 14.41 hectares

5. Area more than once sown – 950.10 hectares

6. Other waste – 71.18 hectares

Reddiarchatram is situated on the Dindigul Palani road with its boundary begining beyond Dindigul. It has a total population of 87,788, of which males are 44,322 and females 43,466 including 15,672 of which males 7,955 and 7,717 females in scheduled castes and scheduled tribes 557 of which 293 males and 264 females segments as per the last census 1991. This block is spread over 147.03 square kilometres. There are about 23 revenue villages covering more than 214 hamlets under 23 village and 2 town panchayats. Totally 82 schools with a higher secondary school followed by 3 secondary cadre serving the block in meeting educational needs. There is one professional college and one technical college. Two primary health centres supported by 12 mini health units are taking care of people's health. Cattle are treated in two veterinary dispensaries and eight sub-centres throughout the block.

In the block, there is union tar road for 9 kms, metal road for 69 kms, stone road for 49 kms and mud road for 17 kms. Panchayat roads of metal, stone and mud types have been laid to a distance of 7 kms, 66 kms and 20 kms respectively. These roads are linking most of the villages and the main roads of major towns. Three railway stations are functioning in the block. Water supply is made available through 293 open wells and 280 hand pumps with the support of 60 overhead and 10 ground level tanks. The total cultivable land is 51622 hectares of which 2061 hectare is wet land and 49561 hectares is dry land. The area of fallow land is about 20728 hectares. Tanks, small ponds and check dams or percolation dams numbering about 160 supply water for agricultural purpose. A ginning factory/spinning mill and 5 tanneries are working in the block. The functioning of commercial institutions such as Land Development Bank (1), Cooperative societies (10), and Primary Agricultural Cooperative Banks (24) and other National Banks is worth mentioning in the process of the development of the block.

Athoor Block is located 16 kms west of Dindigul Town, spread over 135.79 square kilometres. It has a total population of 85,239, of which 42,971 are males and 42,268 females. There are about 21 revenue villages in the block, which covers 114 hamlets and all are attached to 22 village and 3 town panchayats.

This block is served by an Arts College along with a Technical College and 3 each of higher secondary and secondary schools. About 75 elementary and 60 middle schools are also found. The people of this block take reqular treatment in 2 government hospitals and 2 primary health centres. In addition to these, 21 mini health centres are catering to the needs of pregnant mothers and nursing children, while 2 dispensaries and 5 clinics are functioning in the block for cattle care. The tar, metal and mud roads of panchayat union and village panchayats connect various villages and central places in the block. Open wells and hand pumps connected with overhead and ground level tanks facilitate water supply to the people.

A railway station, two police stations, a police outpost and a rural university are notable for their service. Chinnalapatti Town Panchayat in the block is very famous for handlooms and wire chairs. National Banks, Primary Cooperative Banks and Cooperative fair price shops are rendering fruitful service to the people.

Village Profile

The profile of the six villages chosen for the study depends on both secondary and primary information. Demographic details, geographical features and land use pattern have been collected from secondary and documentary sources. On the other hand, details of women employment and harassment in various forms have been obtained from women respondents by personal contact established by the researcher at their homes. The sample villages in these blocks are summarised in this chapter to provide a comprehensive profile of these villages and their people.

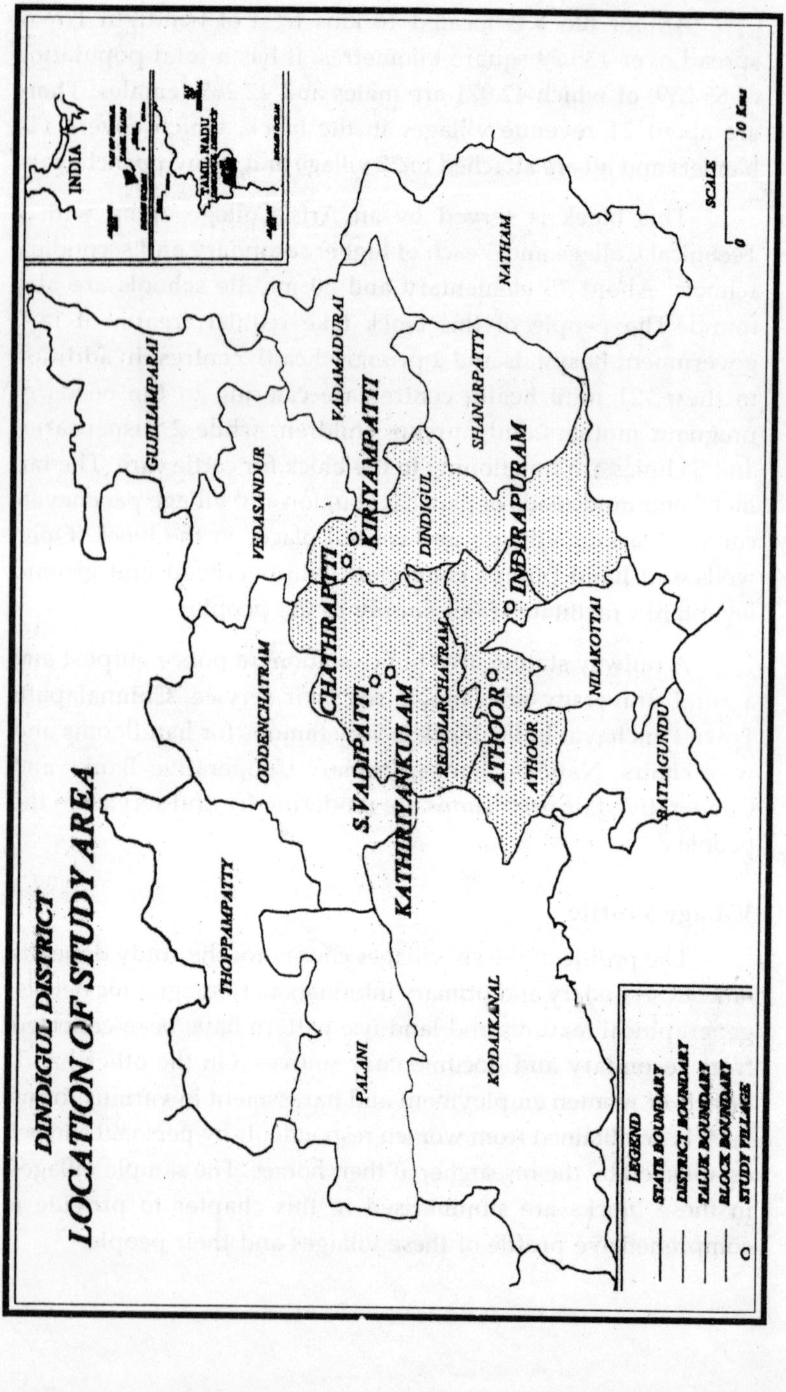
DINDIGUL DISTRICT
LOCATION OF STUDY AREA
INDIA
TAMIL NADU
SCALE
0
10 Kms
GUJILIAMPARAI
VEDASANDUR
VADAMADURAI
NATHAM
KIRIYAMPATTI
CHATHRAPATTI
DINDIGUL
SHANARPATTY
INDIRAPURAM
ODDENCHATRAM
S.VADIPATTI
KATHIRIYANKULAM
REDDIARCHATRAM
ATHOOR
ATHOOR
NILAKOTTAI
BATLAGUNDU
THOPPAMPATTY
PALANI
KODAIKANAL
LEGEND
STATE BOUNDARY
DISTRICT BOUNDARY
TALUK BOUNDARY
BLOCK BOUNDARY
STUDY VILLAGE

The geographical location of the study area can be well appreciated from the map in Figure 1 and the names of the study villages are given in Table 4.2.

Table 4.2. Study Villages

S.No.	Block	Village	
		Developed	Underdeveloped
1.	Athoor	Athoor	Indirapuram
2.	Reddiyarchatram	S.Vadipatti	Kathiriyankulam
3.	Dindigul	Chatrapatti	Kiriyampatti

A set of villages has been taken from each block and each set is classified into developed and underdeveloped. These villages are in three different development blocks of Dindigul District.

Athoor

Athoor village belongs to Athoor Village Panchayat. The total population of Athoor is 6274, of which 3099 are males and 3175 are females and 1452 are Scheduled Caste people. Kamarajar Dam is constructed 5 kms west of this village and it supplies drinking water to Dindigul, Chinnalapatti and its surroundings in addition to Athoor. This village has tanks for irrigation of cultivable lands. Fiscal transaction is the routine work of the Athoor branch of Canara Bank. Cooperative milk societies are in successful operation. Cooperative fair price shops sell consumer goods at subsidised rates. The one post office facilities letter correspondence and communication. Mahalir Mandram and a non-governmental organisation (NGO) motivate that people to right choice. A primary health centre and a mini health centre are maintaining sound health of the village people.

S.Vadipatti

S.Vadipatti village comes under Silvarpatti Village Panchayat with the total households being 133. The total population is 580, of which males are 280 and females 300. The majority of the people in this village belong to Hinduism while a small minority belongs to Christianity. The total geographical area is 97.43 hectares, in which garden land is more than other lands, i.e., 38.48.5 hectares. The major crops raised are cholam, groundnut and pulses. After elementary or primary education the schoolgoers have to come outside the village for any type of higher study. For other necessities the villagers depend on Reddiarchatram and Silvarpatti and for medical facilities they come to Dindigul. Mahalir Mandram is creating awareness about government schemes and welfare measures among all the people in the village.

Chatrapatti

Agaram Town Panchayat includes Chatrapatti Village, which has a total population of 489, comprising 277 males, 212 females and 318 Scheduled Caste population. Dry land is more (65.60.5 hectare) followed by 28.29.6 hectare garden land out of the total geographical area of 110.51.5 hectare. Cholam, cereals and pulses are cultivated as major crops. This village relies on Ulagampatti and Agaram and mostly on Thadikkombu for infrastructure facilities except balwadi and noon meal centre for small children and old age people. The major source of water for irrigation are open wells and a river. People use open sewer as their village toilet. Community television brings them daily news and gives relaxation in their routine life. Well organised Mahalir Mandram, Youth Club and Village Planning Committee are effectively serving the village in getting the agricultural implements and smokeless chhulhas at subsidised rates under ICAR programme and IRDP loan for milch animal, bullock and cart and group houses for Scheduled Caste families.

Indirapuram

Indirapuram village comes under Ambathurai Revenue Village in Athoor Block. Earlier it was called 'Sakkiliapatti' because all the households belong to Scheduled Caste. It is a single caste village. The total population of Indirapuram is 471, of which 240 are males and 231 are females and the total number of households is 85. It is a remote village without any proper tar road and there is no bus transport facility. Bus transport facility is available only from Nadupatti a nearby village. There is one balwadi which looks after the children and it is run by Gandhigram Trust with the assistance of the Social Welfare Board, Tamil Nadu. A primary school is functioning and it is controlled by the Adi Dravida Welfare Department.

Two community wells and one hand borewell supply drinking water through four water taps located in different parts of the village. There is no post office, bank or health centre facilities. To avail themselves of these facilities the villagers have to go to other villages. One Mahalir Mandarm is functioning to empower the rural women.

It has no tanks and the cultivable lands mainly depend upon wells and rainfall. The major crops are cholam, samai, red gram, black gram, cereals and pulses and cash crops like jasmine, pitchippu, jammanki and marugu (flowers) and vegetables like brinjal, onion, drumstick.

Kathiriyankulam

Kathiriyankulam is a Scheduled Caste village having 152 households for its 628 total population with comparatively lesser (284) female population. The total geographical area is 141.94.3 hectare, of which the proportion of dry land is 83.88.8 hectare, followed by garden land 33.54.5 hectare, and, waste land 20.82.5 hectare. Cholam, cotton and sunflower are grown in dry land and sugarcane, vegetables, onion, groundnut and paddy are cultivated in garden and wet lands. The major sources of irrigation are wells and pond. Facilities are available for primary education locally and for higher education outside the village. Open defecation is the practice. Village organisations such as Nyaya Panchayat and Youth Club are playing a very vital role in organising the development process.

Kiriyampatti

Kiriyampatti Village comes under Agaram Panchayat in Dindigul Block. The total population of Kiriyampatti village is 627, of which males are 315 and females 312. The village is a Hindu dominated village. In the study village, the main sources of drinking water are handpumps (3) and community wells (3). There is no proper road and also no bus transport facility to this village.

One primary school is functioning. For secondary and other higher education the students go 5 kms away. There is one Mahalir Mandram functioning well and it has links with other Mahalir Mandrams in the sorrounding villages. There is no post office, bank or health facilities.

Total land available for cultivation is 101.10.56 hectares of which dry land accounts 79.4.18 hectares and wet land is 22.6.38 hectares. The major crops raised in the village are cholam, cereals, chillies, and groundnuts. Most of the lands depend upon rainfall for cultivation. Only a small area is covered by well irrigation.

Summary

The profile has briefly outlines the Dindigul District and the characteristic features of its Blocks and villages in terms of geographical location, demography, land particulars, cropping pattern, irrigation, drinking water facilities, social institutions and transport. These socio-economic factors are informative for identifying the study villages that enable the researcher to carry out the present study

5
Data Analysis

Introduction

The present chapter deals with analysis and interpretation of the collected data for the present study. The collected data were presented in the form of tables and the tables are arranged along with the interpreations. The chapter is divided into four sections viz. (i) Socio-economic conditions of the women labourers; (ii) Problems related to women labourers in their work environment; (iii) Problems related in home management; and, (iv) Level of awareness about the development programmes.

(i) Socio-economic Conditions of the Women Labourers

The study was conducted in six villages of three development blocks, viz., Athoor, Reddiyarchatram and Dindigul Blocks in Dindigul District. Out of the six villages three were developed villages and the remaining three were underdeveloped villages. In each block one developed and one underdeveloped village were selected.The three developed villages were selected on the basis of irrigational facilities available in the villages. The developed villages selected for this study are Athoor, S.Vadipatti and Chatrapatti, and underdeveloped villages are Indirapuram, Kathirayankulam and Kiriyampatti.

The study was conducted among the landless women labourers. Table 5.1 presents the village-wise distribution of the respondents. A total of 500 women respondents were contacted for this study, of which 309 (61.8 per cent) were from the developed villages and 191 (38.2 per cent) were from the underdeveloped villages. The majority of the respondents (62 per cent) belonged to developed villages.

The village-wise number of respondents were: Athoor (152), S.Vadipatti (90), Chatrapatti (67), Indirapuram (65), Kathirayankulam (63), and Kiriyampatti (63).

Table 5.1. Village wise Distribution of Women Labourers

Block	*Village*	*Respondents*
Developed		
Athoor	1. Athoor	152 (30.4)
R. Chatram	2.S.Vadipatti	90 (18.0)
Dindigul	3.Chatrapatti	67 (13.4)
	Total (A)	309 (61.8)
Underdeveloped		
Athoor	1.Indirapuram	65 (13.0)
R. Chatram	2.Kathiriyankulam	63 (12.6)
Dindigul	3.Kirlyampatti	63 (12.6)
	Total (B)	**191 (38.2)**
	Grand Total (A+B)	**500 (100.0)**

Source : Computed from primary data

* Figures in parantheses indicate percentages

Age-wise Distribution

Age is an important factor which determines the physical ability to work as a labourer in the unorganised sector. To understand the working age group, it is necessary to classify the respondents according to their age. Table 5.2 shows the age-wise distribution of the respondents.

The lowest age of the respondent was 15 years and the highest was 70 years. More than three-fifths of them (62.8 per cent) were in the age group of 20-39 years followed by one-fourths (25.2 per cent) who were aged between 40-59 years. There were 40 respondents (8 per cent) aged below 20 years and the remaining 4 per cent were aged above 60 years. Group-wise, there is much difference between the two types of villages: 63.4 per cent of the respondents from the developed villages and 36.6 per cent of those from the underdeveloped villages was 20-39 years. Respondents in the age group of 40-59 years were more (26.9 per cent) in the developed villages than in the underdeveloped villages (22.5 per cent).

There were (12.6 per cent) of the respondents aged below 20 years from the underdeveloped villages, while from the developed villages, there were (5.2 per cent). Also, among the respondents aged above 60 years (4.7 per cent) were from underdeveloped villages and 3.6 per cent from the developed villages.

The majority of the respondents (62.8 per cent) were in the age group of 20-39, years which is an age at which people will be more responsibile. So, it is inferred that the majority of the respondents were in a position to understand their family responsibilities.

Marital Status

Marriage is an institution or complex of social norms that sanctions the relationships of a man and woman and binds them in a system of mutual obligations and rights essential to the functioning of family life. The marriage signifies the recognition by both the husband and wife of their new status in the community

Table 5.2. Age-wise Distribution of Women Labourers

Block	*Village*	*Age*				*Total*
		< 20	*20-39*	*40-59*	*>60*	
	Developed					
Athoor	1. Athoor	5 (3.3)	98 (64.5)	42 (27)	7 (4.5)	152
R.Chatram	2.S.Vadipatti	5 (5.5)	54 (60.0)	28 (31.1)	3 (1.0)	90
Dindigul	3.Chatrapatti	6 (8.9)	47 (70.1)	13 (19.4)	1 (1.6)	67
	Total (A)	16 (5.2)	199 (64.4)	83 (26.9)	11 (3.6)	309 (61.8)
	Underdeveloped					
Athoor	1.Indirapuram	8 (12.3)	38 (58.5)	17 (26.0)	2 (3.0)	65
R.Chatram	2.Kathiriyankulam	8 (8.1)	44 (69.8)	9 (9.9)	2 (3.2)	63
Dindigul	3.Kiriyampatti	8 (12.6)	33 (52.4)	17 (27.0)	5 (8.0)	63
	Total (B)	24 (12.6)	115 (60.2)	43 (22.5)	9 (4.7)	191 (38.2)
	Grand Total (A+B)	40 (8.0)	314 (62.8)	116 (23.2)	20 (4.0)	500 (100.0)

Source : Computed from primary data; * Figures in parantheses indicate percentages

Table 5.3. Marital Status of Women Labourers

Block	Village	Marital Status					Total
		Married	Un married	Widow	Separated	Destitute	
	Developed						
Athoor	1. Athoor	125 (82.5)	7 (4.6)	17 (11.2)	2 (1.3)	1 (6.5)	152
R. Chatram	2. S.Vadipatti	72 (80.0)	7 (7.8)	11 (12.2)	--	--	90
Dindigul	3. Chatrapatti	59 (88.0)	1 (1.5)	5 (7.5)	2 (3.0)	--	67
	Total (A)	256 (82.9)	15 (4.8)	33 (10.7)	4 (1.3)	1 (0.3)	309 (61.8)
	Underdeveloped						
Athoor	1. Indirapuram	51 (78.5)	5 (3.3)	8 (12.3)	1 (1.5)	--	65
R.Chatram	2. Kathiriyankulam	55 (87.3)	2 (3.2)	6 (9.5)	--	--	63
Dindigul	3. Kiriyampatti	53 (84.1)	1 (1.6)	7 (11.1)	2 (3.2)	--	63
	Total (B)	159 (83.2)	8 (4.2)	21 (11.0)	3 (1.6)	--	191 (38.2)
	Grand Total (A+B)	415 (83.0)	23 (4.6)	54 (10.8)	7 (1.4)	1 (0.2)	500 (100.0)

Source : Computed from primary data; * Figures in parantheses indicate percentages

and also signifies the social approval and support of the new status contracted.

In Indian society, marriage is the important ceremony which allows women to get into a new life and status. Normally married women are allowed to go for work and unmarried women are allowed only with some restrictions depending on the socio-cultural and economic condition of the family. Table 5.3 presents the marital status of the study respondents.

More than four-fifths of the respondents (83.0 per cent) were married and 4.6 per cent were unmarried. There were also widows (10.8 per cent) separated women (1.4 per cent) and destitute women (0.2 per cent).

When we compare the marital status of the respondents across the group of villages there seems to be no significant difference.

The majority of the respondents (83 per cent) were married and this is one of the major factors that made the women go for work to support the family economically.

Education Status

Education is an important factor which helps to develop human resources. Empowerment of women can be attained only through education of women and also through creating awareness about their rights and responsibilities. "Education is the process of bringing desirable change into the behaviour of human beings. As society develops, it becomes imperative that the cumulative experience, social and other development should be passed on to new generations, or to the people who need this knowledge. The accepted customs, norms, values, skills, which are required to be preserved need to be passed on to successive generations. It is the need for education that gradually gave rise to a philosophy of education" (Dahama and Bhatnagar,1985). Education of women is key role in a developmental strategy. If women are trained and educated on sound lines, they become an asset in accelerating economic growth and ensuring social change in the desired direction (Immanuel 1998). Mostly manual type of work is done by illiterates and the less educated. Table 5.4 shows the educational status of the respondents.

The highest level of education of the women labourers was secondary school. Among the 500 respondents contacted for this study, 69 per cent were illiterates, (Mass illiteracy is one of the most distressing features among the women labourers of the unorganised sectors of both the States of Bihar and West Bengal (Saran and Sandhwar 1990). 12.0 per cent were literates; the educational level of 12.6 per cent was primary level; and, the remaining 6.4 per cent had studied upto the secondary level.

When we compare the literacy level of the respondents, 73.3 per cent from the underdeveloped villages and 66.3 per cent from the developed villages were illiterates; 14.2 per cent of the respondents from developed villages and 8.4 per cent from underdeveloped villages were literates; and, there is no significant difference among the respondents who have studied upto primary and secondary levels. Thus, the underdeveloped villages had a higher percentage of illiterate respondents (73.3 per cent) than the developed villages (66.3 per cent).

The majority of the respondent women labourers (69 per cent) were illiterates. Group-wise, the underdeveloped villages had higher (73.3 per cent) percentage of illiterates than the developed villages (66.3 per cent). The developed villages have more educational facility than the underdeveloped villages. This is the main reason for higher illiteracy in the underdeveloped villages.

It is inferred that the prevailing illiteracy among these working women in the unorganised sector is the main cause for their being ignorant of their rights and taking steps to make them at least literates will empower them.

Occupational details

Occupation not only determines the employment and income potential of an individual but also indicates his economic and

Table 5.4. Educational Status of Women Labourers

Block	*Village*	*Illiterate*	*Literate*	*Primary*	*Secondary*	*Total*
	Developed					
Athoor	1. Athoor	96 (63.1)	28 (18.4)	21 (13.8)	7 (4.6)	152
R.Chatram	2. S.Vadipatti	68 (75.6)	7 (7.8)	9 (10.0)	6 (6.7)	90
Dindigul	3. Chatrapatti	41 (61.2)	9 (13.4)	10 (14.9)	7 (10.4)	67
	Total (A)	205 (66.3)	44 (14.2)	40 (13.0)	20 (6.5)	309 (61.8)
	Underdeveloped					
Athoor	1. Indirapuram	45 (69.2)	6 (9.2)	7 (10.8)	7 (10.8)	65
R.Chatram	2. Kathiriyankulam	50 (79.4)	---	10 (15.9)	3 (4.8)	63
Dindigul	3. Kiriyampatti	45 (71.4)	10 (15.9)	6 (9.5)	2 (3.2)	63
	Total (B)	140 (73.3)	16 (8.4)	23 (12.0)	12 (6.3)	191 (38.2)
	Grand Total (A+B)	345 (69.0)	60 (12.0)	63 (12.6)	32 (6.4)	500 (100.0)

Source : Computed from primary data; * Figures in parantheses indicate percentages

Figure II
Educational Status of Women Labourers

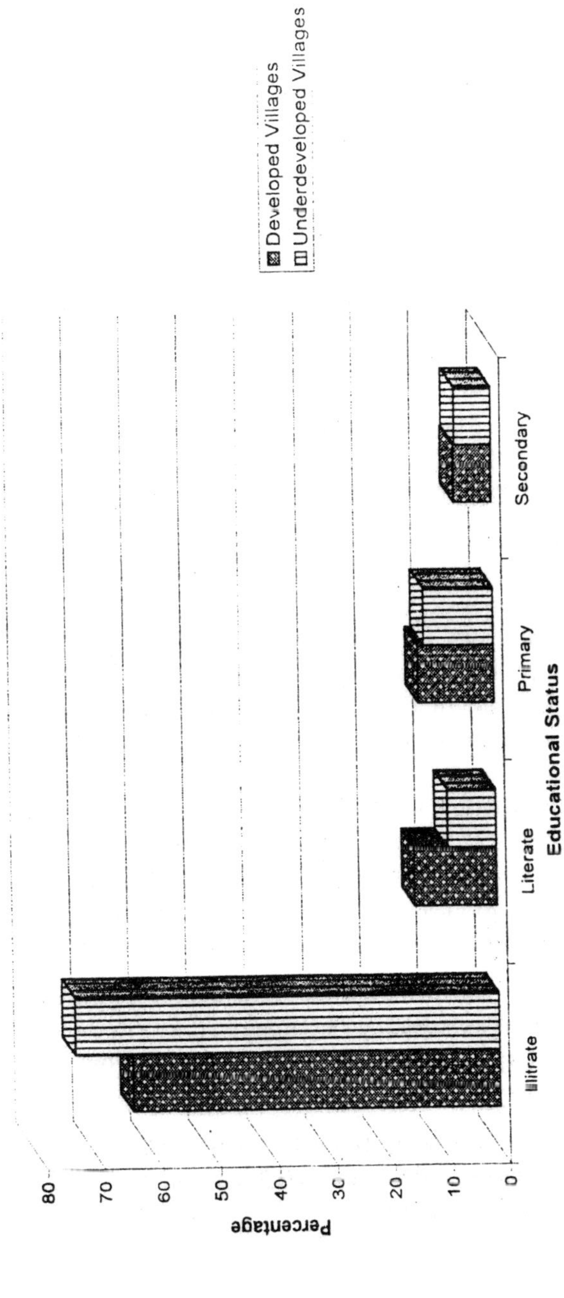

social status as well. In this sense, occupation serves as the link that holds individuals to the social and economic order of a community. But, in the case of women labourers, they are forced to take the occupation as compulsory for their family survival and maintenance. Table 5.5 shows the occupation-wise classification of the women labourers.

The study was conducted among rural landless labourers involved in various types of occupations. More than nine-tenths of these respondents (91.4 per cent) were involved as agricultural labourers. The other types of occupations included brick work (3.2 per cent), construction work (3.0 per cent), mill work (1.2 per cent), labour in the coir industry (0.6 per cent) and labour in the paper board mill (0.6 per cent).

Group-wise, 93.2 per cent of the women from developed villages and 88.5 per cent of those from the underdeveloped villages were agri-labourers. The income from the main occupation was not enough to meet the family expenses.

Also, the women labourers did not get employment throughout the year. So, this situation compelled the women labourers to have some type of subsidiary occupations to supplement their income. Of the total 500 respondents, only 12.4 per cent of them said that they had some type of subsidiary occupations such as agriculture, construction, brick work, mill work and basket-making. Agricultural labour is the subsidiary occupation for 45.1 per cent of the respondents. Another one-third (32.3 per cent) were construction workers while 9.7 per cent were involved in brick work. Paper board mill provided work to 11.3 per cent of the respondents and one respondent (1.6 per cent) was involved in basket-making.

Group-wise, there were more respondents doing agricultural labour as subsidiary occupation (54.8 per cent) from the developed villages whereas more percentage of women labourers (16.1 per cent) from the underdeveloped villages involved in brick work.

The majority of the respondents (91.4 per cent) were agricultural labourers (93.2 per cent from developed villages and 88.5 per cent from underdeveloped villages).

Table 5.5. Occupation-wise Distribution of Women Labourers

Block	Village	Main							Subsidary					
		1	2	3	4	5	6	Total	7	8	9	10	11	Total
	Developed													
Athoor	1. Athoor	145 (95.4)	7 (4.6)	---	---	---	---	152	4 (28.5)	9 (64.3)	1 (7.1)	---	---	14 (9.2)
R.Chatram	2. S.Vadipatti	87 (96.7)	3 (3.3)	---	---	---	---	90	3 (75.0)	1 (25.0)	---	---	---	4 (4.4)
Dindigul	3. Chatrapatti	56 (83.6)	1 (1.4)	3 (4.5)	3 (4.5)	1 (1.4)	3 (4.5)	67	10 (76.9)	---	---	2 (15.4)	1 (7.7)	13 (19.4)
	Total (A)	288 (93.2)	11 (3.5)	3 (1.0)	3 (1.0)	1 (0.3)	3 (1.0)	309 (61.8)	17 (54.8)	10 (32.3)	1 (3.2)	2 (6.4)	1 (3.2)	31 (50.0)
	Underdeveloped													
Athoor	1. Indirapuram	65 (100.0)	---	---	---	---	---	65	---	---	---	---	---	---
R.Chatram	2. Kathiriyankulam	60 (95.2)	2 (3.1)	---	---	1 (1.6)	---	63	1 (12.5)	2 (25.0)	---	5 (62.5)	---	8 (12.7)
Dindigul	3. Kiriyampatti	23 (36.5)	---	---	---	---	---	---	37 (58.7)	3 (4.8)	---	---	---	63
	Total (B)	169 (88.5)	4 (2.1)	13 (6.8)	3 (1.6)	2 (1.0)	---	191 (38.2)	11 (35.5)	10 (32.3)	5 (16.1)	5 (16.1)	---	31 (50.0)
	Grand Total (A+B)	457 (91.4)	15 (3.0)	16 (3.2)	6 (1.2)	3 (00.6)	3 (00.6)	500 (100.0)	28 (45.1)	20 (32.3)	6 (9.7)	7 (11.3)	1 (1.6)	62 (12.4)

Source : Computed from primary data; * Figures in parantheses indicate percentages

1. Agriculture, 2. Construction, 3. Brick Work, 4. Mill Work, 5. Coir Industry, 6. Paper Mill 7. Agriculture, 8. Construction, 9. Brick Work, 10. Mill Work, 11. Coir Industry, 12. Paper Mill

Only 12.4 per cent of the respondents followed subsidiary occupations like agricultural labour, construction work, brick work, paper board mill work and basket-making.

Religion and Caste

With regard to religion, a vast majority (88 per cent) of the women labourers belong to Hindu religion and the remaining (12 per cent) are Christian.

"A very peculiar type of social grouping which is found in India is the caste grouping. Caste largely determines the function, the status, the available opportunities as well as the handicaps for an individual. Caste differences even determine modes of domestic and social life, types of houses and cultural patterns of the people which are found in the rural area. Even land ownership exists frequently on caste lines. Due to a number of reasons, administrative functions have also been often divided according to castes, especially in the rural area" (A.R. Desai 1997). Table 5.6 shows the caste-wise distribution of the women labourers.

Out of the 500 women labourers in the study area, 72.0 per cent belonged to Scheduled Caste. (The women belonging to Scheduled Castes, Scheduled Tribes and Backward Classes are the backbone in brick works and quarries and mines of Bihar and West Bengal. They are 98 per cent and 99 per cent in these unorganised sector in Bihar and 97 per cent and 89 per cent respectively in West Bengal (Saran., A.B. and Sandhwar 1990). 26.6 per cent of the respondents were from backward communities; and, the rest (1.4 per cent) were from Most Backward communities.

Caste-wise, the majority of the respondents (33.2 per cent) were Pallars, followed by 29.2 per cent of Sakkiliars and 9.6 per cent of Parayars. All these castes come under the category of Scheduled Caste. The other caste groups of the respondents included Gowndars (9.4 per cent), Pillaimars (8.4 per cent), Vannars (5.2 per cent), Naickers (2.4 per cent), Asariars (0.6 per cent), Konars (0.6 per cent). All these castes come under the

Table 5.6. Caste-wise Distribution of Women Labourers

Block	Village	Scheduled Caste			Most Backward		Backward Class			
		Sakkiliar	*Pallar*	*Parayar*	*Kallar*	*Vannar*	*Vanniar*	*Pillaimar*	*Gowndar*	*Asariar*
Athoor	**Developed** 1. Athoor	11 (7.2)	36 (23.7)	48 (2.4)	48 (2.4)	---	26 (17.1)	7 (4.6)	5 (3.3)	---
R.Chatram	2. S.Vadipatti	34 (37.8)	36 (40.0)	---	---	---	---	16 (17.8)	4 (4.4)	---
Dindigul	3. Chatrapatti	---	47 (70.1)	---	---	---	---	19 (28.0)	1 (1.5)	---
	Total (A)	45 (14.6)	119 (38.5)	48 (15.5)	4 (1.3)	---	26 (8.4)	42 (13.6)	10 (3.2)	---
Athoor	**Underdeveloped** 1. Indirapuram	65 (100.0)	---	---	---	---	---	---	---	---
R. Chatram	2. Kathiriyankulam	13 (20.6)	47 (74.6)	---	---	3 (4.8)	---	---	---	---
Dindigul	3. Kiriyampatti	23 (36.5)	---	---	---	---	---	---	37 (58.7)	3 (4.8)
	Total (B)	101 (52.9)	47 (24.6)	---	---	3 (1.6)	---	---	37 (19.3)	3 (1.6)
	Grand Total (A+B)	146 (29.2)	165 (33.2)	48 (9.6)	4 (0.8)	3 (0.6)	26 (5.2)	42 (8.4)	47 (9.4)	3 (0.6)

Source : Computed from primary data

* Figures in parantheses indicate percentages

category of Backward Community. Kallars (0.8 per cent) and Vannars (0.6 per cent) come under the Most Backward Community category.

Group-wise the underdeveloped villages had more Scheduled Castes (77.5 per cent) respondents than the developed villages (68.6 per cent). There were more Most Backward Communities (1.6 per cent) in the underdeveloped villages than in the developed villages (1.3 per cent). But the developed villages had a higher percentage of Backward Class respondents (30.1 per cent) than the underdeveloped villages (20.9 per cent). (The Muslim and Christian women workers are negligible in these unorganised sectors (Saran. *Data Analysis* A.B. and Sandhwar 1990).

Family Type and Family Size

Scheduled Caste respondents formed the majority (72 per cent) in the study. This shows that the Scheduled Caste people of these study villages must be guided and helped both economically and employment-wise to come up in their life. Joint family is the traditional family type in most parts of India. Among rural families, especially agricultural families, joint families are quite common. But the modernisation and disintegration of joint family system has paved the way for the emergence of nuclear family system in the rural areas. Table 5.7 shows the distribution of respondents according to their family type.

Group-wise, there is not much difference, where 87.7 per cent of the respondents from developed villages and 84.8 per cent of those from underdeveloped villages came from nuclear families while 15.2 per cent from underdeveloped villages and 12.3 per cent from developed villages belonged to joint families. The percentage of nuclear families was slightly higher (87.7 per cent) in the developed villages whereas the percentage of joint families (15.2 per cent) was slightly higher in the underdeveloped villages. The majority of the respondents (86.6 per cent) came from nuclear families.

Table 5.7. Type of Family among Women Labourers

Block	Village	Family Type		Total
		Nuclear	Joint	
	Developed			
Athoor	1. Athoor	133 (87.5)	19 (12.5)	152
R.Chatram	2.S.Vadipatti	80 (88.9)	10 (11.1)	90
Dindigul	3.Chatrapatti	58 (86.5)	9 (13.4)	67
	Total (A)	271 (87.7)	38 (12.3)	309 (61.8)
	Underdeveloped			
Athoor	1.Indirapuram	56 (86.1)	9 (11.9)	65
R.Chatram	2.Kathiriyankulam	55 (87.3)	8 (12.7)	63
Dindigul	3.Kiriyampatti	51 (81.0)	12 (19.0)	63
	Total (B)	162 (84.8)	29 (15.2)	191 (38.2)
	Grand Total (A+B)	433 (86.6)	67 (13.4)	500 (100.0)

Source: Computed from primary data

* Figures in parantheses indicate percentages.

With regard to the family type of the women labourers, it was noticed that 86.6 per cent of the respondents were from nuclear families whereas the remaining 13.4 per cent came from joint families.

Among the institutions that compose rural society the family is the most important. It has been its very foundation. It plays a decisive role in the material and cultural life of the rural aggregate and in moulding the psychological characteristics of the rural individual as well as the rural collectivity. Traditionally agrarian society encouraged joint family system which had more than ten members in a family. Normally large size families are needed for doing agricultural operations and also it restricts hired labour.

Figure I

Caste-wise Distribution of Women Labourers

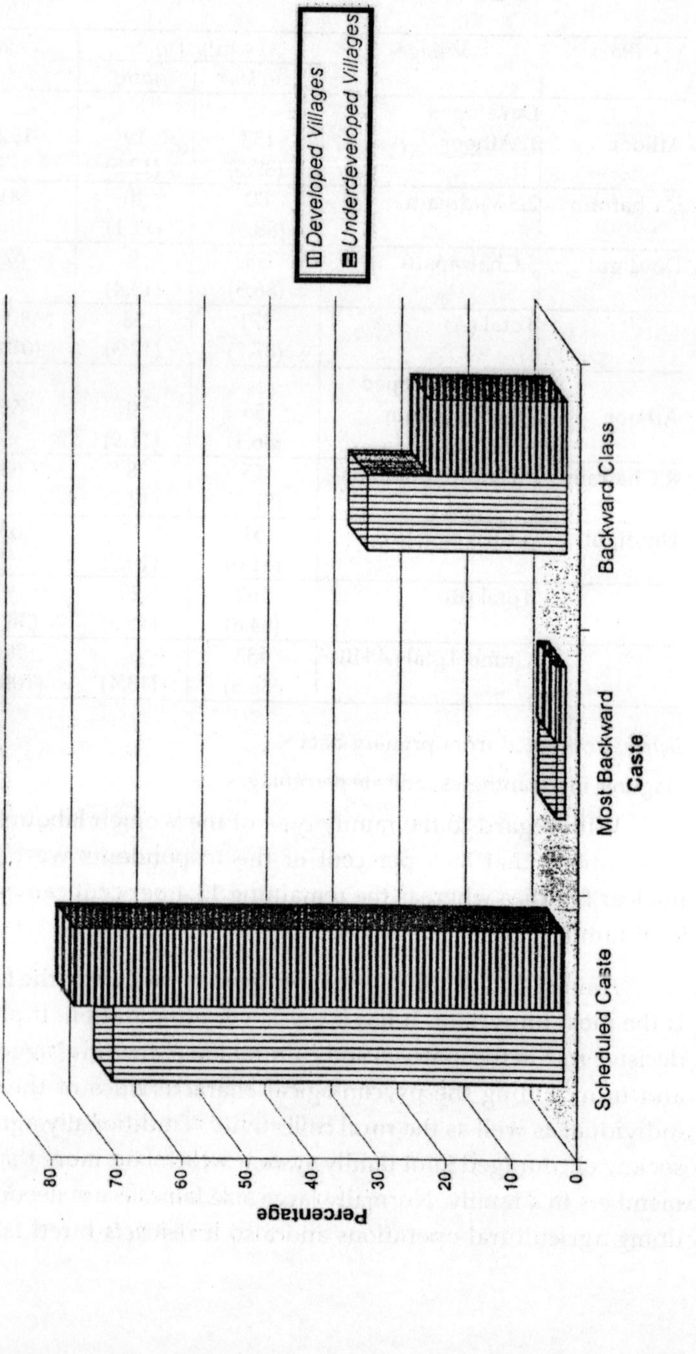

But the emergence of nuclear families in the rural areas, helps to adopt small family norm also.

Table 5.8. Family Size of the Women Labourers

Block	*Village*	*1-5*	*6-8*	*9 and above*	*Total*
	Developed				
Athoor	1. Athoor	120 (79.0)	32 (21.0)	---	152
R.Chatram	2. S.Vadipatti	82 (91.1)	8 (8.9)	---	90
Dindigul	3. Chatrapatti	57 (85.1)	9 (13.4)	1 (1.5)	67
	Total (A)	259 (83.8)	49 (15.9)	1 (0.3)	309 (61.8)
	Underdeveloped				
Athoor	1. Indirapuram	54 (83.0)	11 (17.0)		65
R.Chatram	2. Kathiriyankulam	55 (87.3)	8 (12.7)	---	63
Dindigul	3. Kiriyampatti	55 (87.3)	8 (12.7)	---	63
	Total (B)	164 (85.9)	27 (14.1)	---	191 (38.2)

Source : Computed from primary data

* Figures in parantheses indicate percentages

Table 5.8 shows the family size of the study respondents. The family size of the respondents shows that there are 1-5 members in the majority of the families (84.6 per cent) and the family size is 6-8 in the case of another 15.2 per cent of the respondents, while the remaining one respondent (0.2 per cent) from Chatrapatti, a developed village, has reported the largest family size of 9 members in her family. The same trend of family size is seen both in the developed and the underdeveloped villages, with a slight difference. It is noticed from the table that 85.9 per cent of the families in the underdeveloped villages are having 1-5 members, while the percentage is only 83.8 per cent in the case of the developed villages. On the other hand the larger family size of 6-8 members has been reported by 15.9 per cent of the respondents from the developed villages whereas only 14.1 per cent of those from the underdeveloped villages have reported this size. The inference is that the families in the developed villages have more number of members than those from the underdeveloped villages.

Details of Family Members

Poverty, together with social backwardness traps males and females among agricultural labour households in illiteracy. Among illiterate households enrolment of children in the schools is low and illiteracy gets perpetuated over generations. The lack of education is the root cause of poverty among the landless labourers, especially among women labourers. Table 5.9 shows the total population of the 500 respondent families was 2058, of whom 48.6 per cent were males and the remaining (51.4 per cent) were females. The literacy level of the family members shows that 43.0 per cent of them were illiterates. Of the family members 22.8 per cent had studied upto primary level. The education level of 21.3 per cent of the members was secondary school whereas there were 3.9 per cent literates. The percentage of members who had studied upto higher secondary level was 1.6 per cent and upto college level it was 0.5 per cent. Children below 5 years constituted 7.2 per cent and were also treated as illiterates.

Group-wise, the study families in the developed villages had a total of 1259 members (47.7 per cent males and 52.3 per cent females) and in the underdeveloped villages there were 799 members in the study families with 50.1 per cent males and 49.9 per cent females.

The illiteracy rate was high among the members of underdeveloped villages (43.8 per cent). In the developed villages the percentage of members of literates (4.4 per cent), secondary school level (23.4 per cent), higher secondary (2.0 per cent) was high whereas in the underdeveloped villages the percentage of primary level (24.3 per cent) was high.

Table 5.9. Education and Sex-wise Distribution of Women Labourers' Family Members

Block	Village	Illiterate		Literate		Primary		Secondary		Hr.Secondary		College	
		Male	Female	Male	Female	Male	Female	Male	Female	Male	Female	Male	Female
	Developed												
Athoor	1. Athoor	99 (31.6)	144 (43.4)	6 (1.9)	31 (9.3)	83 (26.5)	76 (22.9)	96 (30.7)	64 (19.3)	10 (3.2)	9 (2.7)	3 (0.9)	---
R.Chatram	2. S.Vadipatti	73 (47.4)	103 (57.0)	---	7 (3.9)	23 (15.0)	37 (20.4)	36 (23.3)	25 (13.8)	28 (1.3)	---	2 (1.6)	---
Dindigul	3. Chatrapatti	42 (31.3)	64 (44.1)	2 (1.5)	9 (6.2)	36 (26.9)	21 (14.5)	37 (27.6)	36 (24.8)	3 (2.2)	1 (0.7)	2 (1.5)	---
	Total (A)	214 (35.6)	311 (47.3)	8 (1.3)	47 (7.1)	142 (23.6)	134 (20.4)	169 (28.1)	125 (19.0)	15 (2.5)	10 (1.5)	7 (1.2)	---
	Underdeveloped												
Athoor	1. Indirapuram	35 (26.5)	72 (53.3)	---	6 (4.4)	47 (35.6)	22 (16.3)	36 (27.3)	19 (14.1)	2 (1.5)	---	1 (1.5)	---
R.Chatram	2. Kathiriyankulam	43 (30.3)	75 (56.0)	1 (0.7)	---	42 (29.6)	31 (23.1)	31 (21.8)	17 (12.7)	4 (2.8)	2 (1.5)	2 (1.4)	---
Dindigul	3. Kiriyampatti	40 (31.7)	85 (65.4)	8 (6.3)	11 (8.5)	32 (25.4)	20 (15.4)	35 (27.8)	7 (5.4)	1 (0.8)	---	---	1 (0.8)
	Total (B)	118 (29.5)	232 (58.1)	9 (2.2)	17 (4.3)	121 (30.2)	73 (18.3)	102 (25.5)	43 (10.7)	7 (1.8)	2 (0.5)	3 (0.8)	1 (0.3)
	Grand Total (A+B)	332 (33.2)	543 (51.4)	17 (1.7)	64 (6.1)	263 (26.3)	207 (19.6)	271 (27.1)	168 (15.9)	22 (2.2)	12 (1.1)	10 (1.0)	1 (0.09)

Source: Computed from primary data

* Figures in parantheses indicate percentages

Among the members of the respondent families, 43 per cent were illiterates and the remaining 57 per cent were literates who had studied up to various levels. This indicates that as the family heads are poor and illiterate, they did not show interest in educating their children or other members of the family, resulting in continued illiteracy.

Occupational classification mainly refers to the classification of working force into different sectoral activities which are taken on the basis of agriculture and allied activities and non-agricultural activities. Table 5.10 shows the occupational classification of family members of the women labourers.

The occupational structure of the respondents family member indicates that three-fourths of the total members (74.3 per cent) were involved in agricultural and allied activities and the remaining 25.7 per cent of the members were engaged in non-agricultural activities.

Group-wise, four-fifths of the family members (80.7 per cent) in the developed villages and 65.5 per cent of those from the underdeveloped villages were agricultural labourers. The members involved in non-agricultural activities included 19.3 per cent from the developed villages and 34.5 per cent from the underdeveloped villages.

Thus, a higher percentage of members from the developed villages were agri-labourers and a higher percentage of non-agricultural labourers (34.5 per cent) were from the underdeveloped villages.

The majority of the family members (74.3 per cent) were involved in agriculture and allied activities. (80.7 per cent from developed villages and 65.5 per cent from underdeveloped villages).

In developed villages the assured irrigation facility provides more employment chances whereas in underdeveloped villages the women labourers have to search for non-agricultural work available in the industrial sector.

Table 5.10. Occupation-wise Classification of Family Members of Women Labourers

Block	Village	Agri	Non-Agri	Total
	Developed			
Athoor	1. Athoor	154 (84.2)	29 (15.8)	183
R.Chatram	2. S.Vadipatti	108 (93.9)	7 (6.1)	115
Dindigul	3. Chatrapatti	60 (59.4)	41 (40.6)	101
	Total (A)	322 (80.7)	77 (19.3)	399 (58.2)
	Underdeveloped			
Athoor	1. Indirapuram	91 (93.8)	6 (6.2)	97
R.Chatram	2. Kathiriyankulam	46 (51.1)	44 (48.9)	90
Dindigul	3. Kiriyampatti	51 (51.0)	49 (49.0)	100
	Total (B)	188 (65.5)	99 (34.5)	287 (41.8)
	Grand Total (A+B)	510 (74.3)	176 (25.7)	686 (100.0)

Source: Computed from primary data

* Figures in paranthesis indicate percentages.

Family Income and Expenditure

Manual labour is a major source of income for the vast majority of people and, for the poor, it is the only source of income. The landless labour households are very poor without any alternative source of income and they have to depend only on their physical labour.

Table 5.11 shows the respondents' monthly family income. The table reveals the fact that among the total respondents 61.1 per cent reported to earn an amount of Rs. 1001-2000 per month, while another 17.2 per cent earn in the range of Rs. 2001-3000. The lowest monthly income of Rs.1000 and less per month has been reported by 16.6 per cent of the respondents whereas the

Table 5.11. Distribution of Women Labourers according to Family Income

Block	*Village*	*Monthly Income (in Rs.)*					
		Below 1000	*1001-2000*	*2001-3000*	*3001-4000*	*Above 4000*	*Total*
	Developed						
Athoor	1. Athoor	31 (20.5)	96 (63.2)	18 (11.8)	4 (2.6)	3 (1.9)	152
R.Chatram	2. S.Vadipatti	20 (22.2)	52 (57.8)	16 (17.8)	1 (1.1)	1 (1.1)	90
Dindigul	3. Chatrapatti	6 (9.0)	41 (61.2)	15 (22.3)	5 (7.5)	---	67
	Total (A)	57 (18.4)	189 (61.2)	49 (15.9)	10 (3.2)	4 (1.3)	309 (61.8)
	Underdeveloped						
Athoor	1. Indirapuram	7 (10.8)	42 (64.6)	11 (16.9)	3 (4.6)	2 (3.1)	65
R. Chatram	2. Kathiriyankulam	6 (9.5)	43 (68.2)	13 (2.7)	1 (1.6)	---	63
Dindigul	3. Kiriyampatti	13 (20.6)	34 (54.0)	13 (20.6)	1 (1.6)	2 (3.2)	63
	Total (B)	26 (13.6)	119 (62.3)	37 (19.4)	5 (2.6)	4 (2.1)	191 (38.2)
	Grand Total (A+B)	83 (16.6)	308 (61.1)	86 (17.2)	15 (3.0)	8 (1.6)	500 (100.0)

Source: Computed from primary data

* Figures in parantheses indicate percentages

Figure III
Distribution of Women Labourers according to Family Income

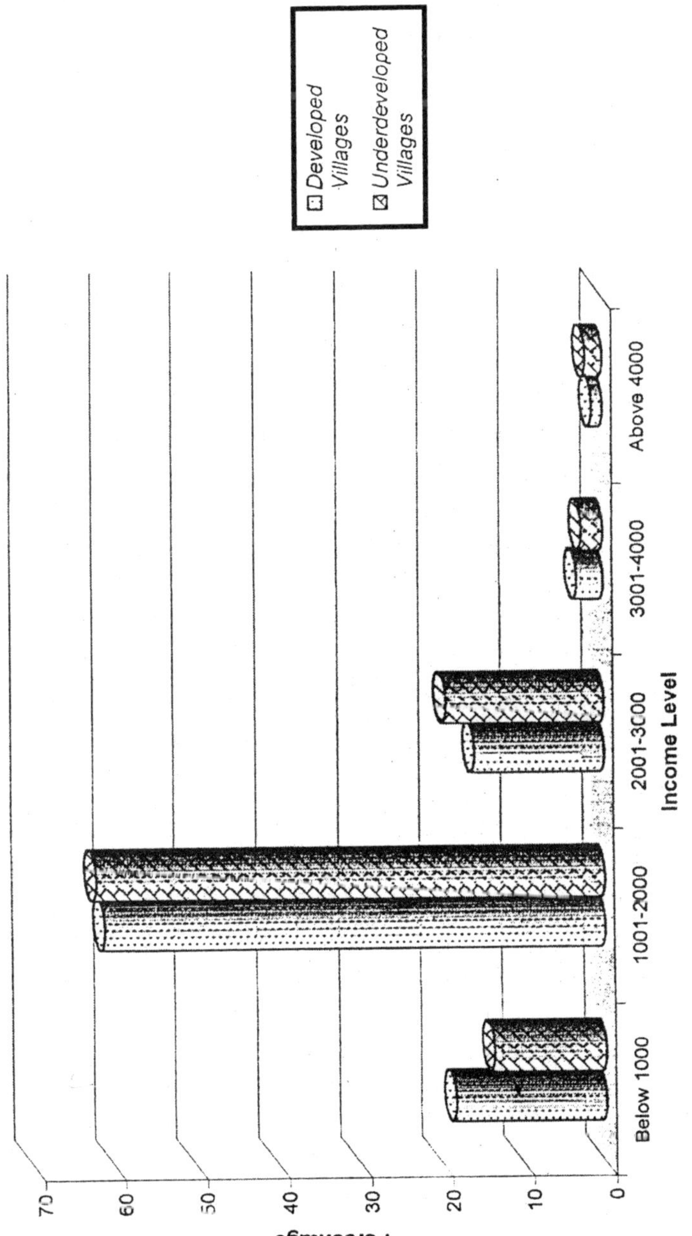

highest amount of Rs. 4000 and above has been reported, by 1.6 per cent of the total respondents.

The economic status of the rural family mainly depends upon the income of the family. Family income determines the purchasing power and the standard of living of the people. In the case of labourers families, family income plays a vital role in acquiring the necessities of life.

The highest amount of Rs. 4000 and above per month has been reported by 2.5 per cent of the respondents from the underdeveloped villages whereas the same range of income is reported by 1.3 per cent of the respondents from the developed villages. The lowest income of Rs.1000 per month has been reported by 18.4 per cent respondents from the developed villages, whereas the percentage is only 13.6 in the underdeveloped villages. The same trend is seen in the other income range also, i.e., in the income range of Rs.1001-2000, 62.3 per cent in underdeveloped villages, as compared to 61.2 per cent in developed villages and, Rs.2001-3000 was reported in the case of underdeveloped villages by 19.4 per cent as against by 15.9 per cent in developed villages. The income is higher in the underdeveloped villages because the respondents' families from these villages are engaged in non-form work that gives them a higher range of income per day. Also, these workers get employment for more number of days.

Overall the monthly income of the majority of the respondent families (62 per cent) is in the range of Rs.1000-2000. Group-wise, the income is higher in underdeveloped villages because, the respondent families from these villages are engaged in non-form work that gives them a higher and regular income.

The majority of the landless labourers are very poor and their income is very low. They are unable to earn more due to inadequate employment opportunities in the unorganised sector. Poor income leads to low standard of living and their expenditure generally exceeds their earnings. Table 5.12 presents the distribution of women labourers according to their monthly family expenditure.

Table 5.12. Monthly Family Expenditure of Women Labourers

Block	*Village*	*Expenditure (in Rs)*			
		Below 1000	*1001-2000*	*2001-3000*	*Total*
	Developed				
Athoor	1. Athoor	58 (38.1)	90 (59.2)	4 (2.7)	152
R.Chatram	2. S.Vadipatti	34 (37.8)	54 (60.0)	2 (2.2)	90
Dindigul	3. Chatrapatti	18 (26.9)	47 (70.1)	2 (3.0)	67
	Total (A)	110 (35.6)	191 (61.8)	8 (2.6)	309 (61.2)
	Underdeveloped				
Athoor	1. Indirapuram	15 (23.0)	48 (73.8)	2 (3.1)	65
R.Chatram	2. Kathiriyankulam	2 (3.2)	57 (90.5)	4 (6.3)	63
Dindigul	3. Kiriyampatti	22 (34.9)	41 (65.1)	---	63
	Total (B)	39 (20.4)	146 (76.4)	6 (3.2)	191 (38.2)
	Grand Total (A+B)	149 (29.8)	337 (67.4)	14 (2.8)	500 (100.0)

Source: Computed from primary data

* Figures in parantheses indicate percentages

Table 5.13 : Housing Condition of Women Labourers

Block	*Village*	*Ownership*					*Conditions*			
		a	*b*	*c*	*d*	*Total*	*e*	*f*	*g*	*Total*
	Developed									
Athoor	1. Athoor	111 (73.0)	18 (11.8)	23 (15.2)	---	152	22 (14.5)	79 (52.0)	51 (33.5)	152
R.Chatram	2. S.Vadipatti	82 (91.1)	2 (2.2)	5 (5.5)	1 (1.1)	90	28 (31.1)	45 (51.1)	16 (17.8)	90
Dindigul	3. Chatrapatti	53 (79.1)	2 (2.9)	10 (14.9)	2 (3.0)	67	23 (34.3)	39 (58.2)	5 (7.5)	67
	Total (A)	246 (79.6)	22 (7.1)	38 (12.3)	3 (1.0)	309 (61.8)	73 (23.6)	164 (53.1)	72 (23.3)	309 (61.8)
	Underdeveloped									
Athoor	1. Indirapuram	61 (93.8)	---	4 (6.2)	---	65	3 (4.6)	54 (83.1)	8 (12.3)	65
R.Chatram	2. Kathiriyankulam	60 (95.2)	---	2 (3.2)	1 (1.6)	63	---	50 (79.4)	13 (20.6)	63
Dindigul	3. Kiriyampatti	48 (76.2)	---	11 (17.5)	4 (6.3)	63	23 (36.5)	29 (46.0)	11 (17.5)	63
	Total (B)	169 (88.5)	---	17 (8.9)	5 (2.6)	191 (38.2)	26 (13.6)	133 (69.6)	32 (16.8)	191 (38.2)
	Grand Total (A+B)	415 (83.0)	22 (4.4)	55 (11.0)	8 (1.6)	500 (100.0)	99 (19.8)	297 (59.4)	104 (20.8)	500 (100.0)

Block	Village	Roof				Structure				
		h	i	j	Total	k	l	m	n	Total
	Developed									
Athoor	1 Athoor	36 (23.7)	64 (42.1)	52 (34.2)	152	31 (21.4)	75 (49.3)	35 (23.0)	11 (7.3)	152
R.Chatram	2. S.Vadipatti	42 (46.7)	48 (53.3)	---	90	44 (48.9)	6 (6.7)	4 (4.4)	36 (40.0)	90
Dindigul	3. Chatrapatti	14 (20.9)	50 (74.6)	3 (4.5)	67	9 (13.4)	32 (47.8)	16 (24.0)	10 (14.9)	67
	Total (A)	92 (29.8)	162 (52.4)	55 (17.8)	309 (61.8)	84 (27.2)	113 (36.6)	55 (17.8)	57 (18.4)	309 (61.8)
	Underdeveloped									
Athoor	1. Indirapuram	6 (9.2)	58 (89.2)	1 (1.5)	65	15 (23.1)	33 (50.1)	3 (4.6)	14 (21.4)	65
R.Chatram	2. Kathiriyankulam	2 (3.2)	56 (90.5)	4 (6.4)	63	5 (7.9)	48 (76.2)	5 (9.5)	4 (6.4)	63
Dindigul	3. Kiriyampatti	12 (19.1)	47 (74.6)	4 (6.3)	63	2 (3.2)	36 (57.1)	16 (25.4)	9 (14.3)	63
	Total (B)	20 (10.5)	162 (84.8)	9 (4.7)	191 (38.2)	22 (11.5)	117 (61.3)	25 (13.1)	27 (14.1)	191 (38.2)
	Grand Total (A+B)	112 (22.4)	324 (64.3)	64 (12.8)	500 (100.0)	106 (21.2)	230 (46.0)	80 (16.0)	84 (16.8)	500 (100.0)

Source: Computed from primary data

* Figures in parantheses indicate percentages

a. own b. leased c c..rented d.construct/govt. e.good f.moderate g.dilapidated h.thatched i.kutcha j.terraced k. hut l. leased m. pucca n. mixed

The monthly expenditure of the women labourer families fluctuates between Rs.300 and Rs.3000. It is observed from the table that the expenditure of 67.4 per cent of the families come to Rs.1001-Rs.2000 per month and, in case of another 29.8 per cent, the monthly family expenditure is less than Rs.1000. The highest expenditure range of Rs.2001-Rs.3000 per month has been reported by a meagre 2.8 per cent of the respondents.

The majority of the families in all the villages, (from 59.2 per cent to 90.5 per cent) have reported to be spending an amount of Rs.1000 Rs.2000 per month. The lowest amount of expenditure of Rs.1000 or less has been reported by 38.1 per cent in Athoor, 37.8 per cent in S.Vadipatti, 34.9 per cent in Kiriyampatti, 26.9 per cent in Chatrapatti and 23.0 per cent in Indirapuram and 3.2 per cent in Kathiriyankulam.

A group-wise analysis of the table also reveals that, among the respondents from the developed villages, 61.81 per cent spent an amount of Rs.1001-Rs.2000 per month while another 35.59 per cent spent Rs.1000 and less. In the underdeveloped villages more than three-fourths (76.4 per cent) spent Rs.1001-Rs. 2000 per month and another one-fifths (20.4 per cent) reported to be spending an amount of Rs. 1000 and less per month. The expenditure data clearly reflected the income data of the women labourers, because, in economic terms, the expenditure of an individual is a function of the levels of income, particularly the disposable income. A comparative analysis the table reveals that the majority of women labourers spending an amount of Rs.1001-Rs.2000 is seen from the underdeveloped villages (76.43 per cent). The number who reported to be spending less than Rs.1000 per month is more (35.59 per cent) from the developed villages than from underdeveloped villages (20.4 per cent). The majority of the study families (67 per cent) spent Rs.1001-Rs.2000 per month. A higher percentage of families (35.6 per cent) from the developed villages spend less than Rs.1000 per month whereas the percentage of such families in the underdeveloped villages was 20.4 percent.

Household Conditions

The problem of housing in India is a complex one. It is quantitatively alarming and qualitatively depressing. Housing conditions in urban as well as rural areas are extremely unsatisfactory. The situation in the rural areas is no better. Though nature has provided them with beautiful air, light and other gifts, the rural people are not taking advantage of them. Instead they live in dark, congested areas and other over-crowded kutcha houses. This situation is largely attributable to ignorance, poverty, sense of insecurity and age-old habits (Chandramouli 1996).

Table 5.13 shows the housing condition of the women labourers. More than 83 per cent of the women labourers lived in their own houses while 11.0 per cent lived in rented houses. Another 4.4 per cent had leased houses and the remaining 1.6 per cent had houses constructed by the government. Group-wise, the majority of the women labourers (88.5 per cent) from underdeveloped and 79.6 per cent from developed villages lived in their own houses. The financial position facilitated 7.1 per cent of the women labourers from the developed villages to lease houses whereas nobody from the underdeveloped villages had this facility. But 2.6 per cent of the women labourers from the underdeveloped villages as against 1.0 per cent of these from the developed villages had been provided with housing facility by the government.

As for the structure of the house, 46.0 per cent were kutcha type whereas 21.2 per cent were huts. There were only 16.0 per cent pucca houses. The majority of the respondents (61.3 per cent) from underdeveloped villages and 36.6 per cent from developed villages lived in kutcha type of houses.

The roofing condition of the houses shows that 64.8 per cent were tiled houses (84.8 per cent from underdeveloped villages and 52.4 per cent from developed villages). The terraced houses account for 12.8 per cent (17.8 per cent from developed villages and 4.7 per cent from underdeveloped villages).

As for the general condition of the houses a little less than three-fourths of them (59.4 per cent) were moderate (69.6 per cent from underdeveloped villages and 53.1 per cent from developed villages).

Whether small or large, the majority of the respondents (83 per cent) owned houses which showed that the women members in the family helped a lot to supplement the family income which helps to save and create assets.

Of the respondents, 46 per cent live in kutcha type of houses; 64.8 per cent of the houses were tiled; 59.4 per cent of the houses were moderate. Some of the houses (104 - 20.8 per cent) in the study area were in dilapidated condition. This clearly indicated that the economic status of the women labourers and the income earned by them even could not meet their daily needs. Under this situation it is very difficult for such women labourers to repair their houses which are in bad shape.

Assets and Liabilities

Asset is a factor which determines the economic position and societal value of one's family. In India, the so-called higher caste people have more assets. But the backward communities like Scheduled Caste groups are assetless. The majority of the landless labourers belong to this category.

The value of assets owned by the women labourers is showm in Table 5.14. It is clear from the table that the value of assets owned by 25.6 per cent of the women labourers ranges between Rs. 5001 and Rs.10000 and where as another 23.8 per cent own assets worth less than Rs. 5000. The highest value of assets has been reported to be Rs. 20000 and above by 19.4 per cent of the respondents.

Village-wise the number of respondents possessing assets of the highest value of Rs. 20000 and above is seen in three villages, namely Kathiriyankulam (28.6 per cent), Kiriyampatti (42.8 per cent) (both underdeveloped villages) and Chatrapatti (44.8 per cent).

Table 5.14. Distribution of Women Labourers according to their Asset Value (in Rs)

Block	Village	Below 5000	5001-10000	10001 - 15000	15001 - 20000	Above 20000	Total
	Developed						
Athoor	1. Athoor	56 (36.8)	56 (36.8)	17 (11.2)	13 (8.5)	10 (6.6)	152
R.Chatram	2. S.Vadipatti	26 (28.9)	24 (26.7)	20 (22.2)	11 (12.2)	9 (10.0)	90
Dindigul	3. Chatrapatti	9 (13.4)	8 (11.9)	13 (19.4)	7 (10.4)	30 (44.8)	67
Total (A)		91 (29.4)	88 (28.5)	50 (16.2)	31 (10.0)	49 (15.9)	309 (61.8)
	Underdeveloped						
Athoor	1. Indirapuram	15 (23.1)	23 (35.4)	18 (27.7)	6 (9.2)	3 (4.6)	65
R.Chatram	2. Kathiriyankulam	5 (7.9)	8 (12.7)	18 (28.6)	14 (22.2)	18 (28.6)	63
Dindigul	3. Kiriyampatti	8 (12.7)	9 (14.3)	11 (17.5)	8 (12.7)	27 (42.8)	63
	Total (B)	28 (14.7)	40 (20.9)	47 (24.6)	28 (14.7)	48 (25.1)	191 (38.2)
	Grand Total (A+B)	119 (23.8)	128 (25.6)	97 (19.4)	59 (11.8)	97 (19.4)	500 (100.0)

Source: Computed from primary data

* Figures in parantheses indicate percentages

Group-wise, those who possess a higher value of assets are more in underdeveloped villages: Rs.10001-Rs.15000 by 24.6 per cent as against 16.2 per cent Rs. 15001-Rs. 20000 by 14.7 per cent as against 10.0 per cent, and, Rs. 20000 and above by 25.1 per cent as against 15.9 per cent. Those who own lesser value of assets are more in number in developed villages, 29.4 per cent as against 14.7 per cent in the group of Rs. 5000 and less and 28.5 per cent as against 20.9 per cent in the category of Rs. 5001-10000. The value of assets owned by 49.4 per cent of the families is less than Rs.10,000.

Group-wise, the families from the underdeveloped villages own assets of a higher value than the families of the developed villages. This may support the earlier findings that the families from the underdeveloped villages used to earn more, spent less and so were able to save and create assets. In developed villages, the respondents were more accustomed to spend on luxury or lavish items and also they mostly depended upon agriculture and allied work in which they did not get higher wages, whereas, in underdeveloped villages, because of less accessibility to town, they spent less and they were engaged mostly in non-agricultural work like brick kiln, mill work, paper board, and coir industry in which they were paid more wages. There are conditions to earn more and spend less. Therefore they were able to save and create assets. The various sources from which the rural labourers borrow loans can be classified into two groups, viz. non-institutional agencies and institutional agencies. The rural landless labourers used to approach village moneylenders and their landlords to get loans. But the institutional agencies meet only a meager portion of their needs, because the landless labourers have little access to institutional credit, except under target-oriented programmes, and pay a high price for consumption credit. Table 5.15 shows the sources of debt of the respondent families.

Among the 500 women labourers contacted for this study, 188 (37.6 per cent) have borrowed money from various sources

Table 5.15. Sources of Debt

Block	Village	No.of Borrowers	No.of Non-Borrowers	Bank	Co-op Societies	Money Lender	Relatives	Friends
	Developed							
Athoor	1. Athoor	48 (31.5)	104 (68.5)	4 (10.5)	2 (5.3)	36 (94.7)	13 (34.2)	4 (10.5)
R.Chatram	2. S.Vadipatti	33 (36.7)	57 (63.3)	1 (3.0)	3 (9.1)	22 (66.7)	19 (57.6)	7 (21.2)
Dindigul	3. Chatrapatti	27 (40.1)	40 (59.9)	4 (14.8)	1 (3.7)	13 (48.1)	12 (44.4)	---
Total (A)		108 (34.9)	201 (65.1)	9 (8.3)	6 (5.6)	71 (65.7)	44 (40.7)	11 (10.2)
	Underdeveloped							
Athoor	1. Indirapuram	23 (35.4)	42 (64.6)	6 (4.3)	---	9 (39.1)	9 (39.1)	---
R.Chatram	2. Kathiriyankulam	22 (34.9)	41 (65.1)	1 (4.5)	69 (27.3)	7 (31.8)	9 (40.9)	---
Dindigul	3. Kiriyampatti	35 (55.0)	28 (45.0)	3 (8.6)	1 (2.8)	24 (68.6)	11 (31.4)	4 (11.4)
	Total (B)	80 (41.9)	111 (58.1)	10 (12.5)	7 (8.8)	40 (50.0)	29 (36.2)	4 (5.0)
	Grand Total (A+B)	188 (37.6)	312 (62.4)	19 (10.6)	13 (7.7)	111 (62.4)	73 (40.1)	15 (8.4)

Source: Computed from primary data

* Figures in parantheses indicate percentages(Multiple responses)

to meet their family and other expenses. Moneylenders form the main source to 111 respondents (62.4 per cent). The other sources of borrowing included relatives (40.1 per cent), banks (10.6 per cent), friends (8.4 per cent) and cooperative societies (7.7 per cent).

Village-wise, moneylenders were the main source of borrowing in all the villages, more particularly in Athoor (94.7 per cent), S.Vadipatti (66.7 per cent), both developed villages, and Kiriyampatti (68.6 per cent). Relatives were also a major source for 57.6 per cent of the women labourers in S.Vadipatti, Chatrapatti (44.4 per cent), both (developed villages) and Kathiriyankulam (40.9 per cent) which comes under the category of underdeveloped villages.

A comparative analysis shows that 34.9 per cent of the respondents in developed villages and 41.9 per cent in underdeveloped villages have borrowed money. A higher percentage of respondents (65.7 per cent) in developed have sought the money lenders as against only 50 per cent in underdeveloped villages.

Moneylenders (62.4 per cent), relatives (40.1 per cent), banks (10.6 per cent) and cooperative societies (7.7 per cent) are the sources of borrowing. Institutional sources like banks and co-operative societies have been used only by a meagre 17.0 per cent of the borrowers which explains the need for motivating them to make use of such sources to avoid exploitation by the moneylenders. These institutional sources should not insist upon a number of rules and regulations to provide loan to these women labourers.

Lack of finance has been the bane of the Indian agricultural and other rural labourers. Indian rural labourers, specially landless labourers, have been traditionally a poor lot, who incur loans not only for investment in house construction and other productive investments but also for bare subsistence and for the fulfilment of social and religious obligations.

Borrowing money for various purposes has become a general habit among the people. Table 5.16 indicates the monetary debt of the respondent families. Among the study respondents, it was reported that 37.6 per cent have borrowed money; 43.1 per cent of the borrowers reported that they got less than Rs. 2500; the amount borrowed falls between Rs. 2501 and Rs. 5000 in the case of 25 per cent; and, the highest amount of Rs. 7500 and above has been reported by 23.9 per cent of the women labourers.

Group-wise, 57.4 per cent of the women labourers from developed villages and 42.6 per cent from underdeveloped villages have borrowed money. The lowest amount of Rs. 2500 and less has been reported by 49.1 per cent of the respondents from the developed villages whereas the highest amount of Rs.7500 and above has been borrowed by 32.5 per cent of the women labourers from the underdeveloped villages. With regard to the purpose of borrowing, family expenses has been reported by 52.6 per cent of the respondents (60.2 per cent in the case of developed villages and 42.6 per cent from the underdeveloped villages). Buying milch animal is the purpose stated by 14.9 per cent of the respondents (23.7 per cent from the underdeveloped villages and 8.3 per cent from the developed villages). The other purpose of borrowing includes construction of houses (12.2 per cent, 15.0 per cent from underdeveloped villages and 10.2 per cent from developed villages), medical expenses (9.6 per cent, 11.2 per cent from underdeveloped villages and 8.3 per cent from developed villages).

With regard to balance amount to be repaid, the majority of the borrowers (50.5 per cent) have reported to have a balance of Rs. 2500 and less. The amount to be repaid by another 21.8 per cent of them ranges between Rs. 2501 and 5000. The highest amount of Rs. 7500 and above has to be repaid by 14.4 per cent of the borrowers.

Group-wise, 55.6 per cent of the borrowers from the developed villages and 43.7 per cent from the underdeveloped

Table 5.16. Details Regarding Monetary Debt

Block	Village	1	Amount (in Rs)				Purpose *							Balance (in Rs)			
			2	3	4	5	6	7	8	9	10	11	12	13	14	15	16
	Developed																
Athoor	1. Athoor	48	29 (60.4)	10 (20.8)	2 (4.2)	7 (14.6)	4 (8.3)	1 (2.1)	37 (77.1)	5 (10.4)	1 (2.1)	1 (2.1)	2 (4.2)	32 (66.7)	10 (20.8)	4 (8.3)	2 (4.2)
R.Chatram	2. S.Vadipatti	33	11 (33.3)	10 (30.3)	5 (15.2)	7 (21.1)	3 (9.1)	5 (15.2)	16 (48.5)	1 (3.0)	4 (12.1)	---	---	13 (39.4)	10 (30.3)	7 (21.2)	3 (9.1)
Dindigul	3. Chatrapatti	27	13 (48.1)	8 (29.6)	1 (3.7)	5 (18.5)	2 (7.4)	3 (11.1)	12 (44.4)	5 (18.5)	4 (14.8)	---	---	15 (55.6)	6 (22.2)	2 (7.4)	4 (14.8)
	Total (A)	108 (57.4	53 (49.1)	28 (25.9)	8 (7.4)	19 (17.6)	9 (8.3)	9 (8.3)	65 (60.2)	11 (10.2)	9 (8.3)	1 (0.9)	2 (1.8)	60 (55.6)	26 (24.1)	13 (12.0)	9 (8.3)
	Underdeveloped																
Athoor	1. Indirapuram	23	10 (43.5)	7 (30.4)	1 (4.3)	5 (21.7)	5 (21.7)	4 (17.4)	8 (34.8)	2 (8.7)	1 (4.3)	1 (4.3)	3 (13.0)	12 (52.2)	8 (34.8)	---	3 (13.0)
R.Chatram	2. Kathiriyankulam	22	5 (22.7)	4 (18.2)	3 (13.6)	10 (45.4)	7 (31.8)	1 (4.5)	7 (31.8)	3 (13.6)	1 (4.5)	4 (18.2)	---	7 (31.8)	7 (31.8)	2 (9.1)	6 (27.3)
Dindigul	3. Kiriyampatti	35	13 (37.1)	8 (22.8)	3 (8.6)	11 (31.4)	7 (20.0)	4 (11.4)	19 (54.3)	7 (20.0)	1 (2.8)	---	4 (11.4)	16 (45.7)	6 (17.1)	4 (11.4)	9 (25.7)
	Total (B)	80 (42.6)	28 (35.0)	19 (23.7)	7 (8.8)	26 (32.5)	19 (23.7)	9 (11.3)	34 (42.6)	12 (15.0)	3 (3.7)	5 (6.3)	7 (8.8)	35 (43.7)	21 (26.3)	6 (7.5)	18 (22.5)
	Grand Total (A+B)	188 (100.0	81 (43.1)	47 (25.0)	15 (7.9)	45 (23.9)	28 (14.9)	18 (9.6)	99 (52.6)	23 (12.2)	12 (6.4)	6 (3.2)	9 (4.8)	95 (50.5)	47 (21.8)	19 (10.1)	27 (14.4)

Source: Computed from primary data * Figures in parantheses indicate percentages(Multiple responses)

1. No. of Respondents, 2. Below 2500, 3. 2500-500, 4. 5000-7500, 5. Above 7500, 6. Milch Animal, 7. Medicial Expense, 8. Family Expense, 9. House Construction, 10. Business Purpose, 11. Education 12. Marriage Loan, 13. Below 2500, 14. 2500-5000, 15. 5000-7500, 16. Above 7500

villages have to repay an amount less than Rs.2500. The highest amount of Rs.7500 and above has to be repaid by 22.5 per cent of the borrowers from underdeveloped villages and 8.3 per cent from the developed villages.

Among the total respondents, 37.6 per cent have borrowed money (57.4 per cent from developed and 42.6 per cent from underdeveloped villages), for various purposes like meeting family expenses, constructing houses, purchase of milch animals etc.

Among the borrowers, 43.1 per cent have borrowed only less than Rs. 2500 which means that the respondent families, provided with assured and regular employment opportunities, will not borrow any money in future.

Share in Family Income

Indian families' major share of the family income is earned by their males members and most of the females are housewives, especially in the high caste families, whereas, in low caste families, both males and females have to earn for their survival. This is more common in the rural areas. The income share of the women labourers in the total family income is presented in Table 5.17. It is observed from the table that 58.2 per cent of the women labourers contribute 25 to 49 per cent of the family income; another 28.6 per cent have stated that their contribution to family income was upto 25 per cent of the total family income; 50 to 74 per cent of the family income was contributed by 5.8 per cent of the women labourers; and, the highest share of 75 to 100 per cent was contributed by 7.4 per cent of the women labourers. Group-wise, among the women labourers of developed villages, 57.6 per cent reported contributing 25 to 49 per cent of their family income while a little above one-fourth (27.8 per cent) contributed less than 25 per cent of the total family income. Among the respondents of underdeveloped villages, the majority (59.2 per cent) contributed 25 to 49 percent of the family income and another 29.8 per cent contributed less than 25 per cent of the family income.

Table 5.17. Women Labourers' Income Share to Total Family Income

Block	*Village*	*Share of Income (%)*				
		Below 25	*25 - 49*	*50 - 74*	*75 - 100*	*Total*
	Developed					
Athoor	1. Athoor	31 (20.4)	104 (68.4)	5 (3.3)	12 (7.9)	152
R.Chatram	2. S.Vadipatti	18 (20.0)	52 (57.8)	10 (11.1)	10 (11.1)	90
Dindigul	3. Chatrapatti	37 (55.2)	22 (32.8)	4 (6.0)	4 (6.0)	67
	Total (A)	86 (27.8)	178 (57.6)	19 (6.2)	26 (8.4)	309 (61.8)
	Underdeveloped					
Athoor	1. Indirapuram	17 (26.1)	44 (67.7)	2 (3.1)	2 (3.1)	65
R.Chatram	2. Kathiriyankulam	20 (31.7)	39 (61.9)	2 (3.2)	2 (3.2)	63
Dindigul	3. Kiriyampatti	20 (31.8)	30 (47.6)	6 (9.5)	7 (11.1)	63
	Total (B)	57 (29.8)	113 (59.2)	10 (5.2)	11 (5.8)	191 (38.2)
	Grand Total (A+B)	143 (28.6)	291 (58.2)	29 (5.8)	37 (7.4)	500 (100.0)

Source: Computed from primary data

* Figures in parantheses indicate percentages(Multiple responses)

A comparative analysis of the table shows that 57.6 per cent of women labourers contributed 25 to 49 percent of the family income. It is more (59.2 per cent) among the respondents in underdeveloped villages. But in case of the contribution of, i.e, 50 to 74 per cent of income the number of respondents is more (6.2 per cent) in the underdeveloped villages than the developed villages.

The majority (58.2 per cent) of the women labourers contributed 25 to 49 per cent of their family income. Group-wise, 58.2 per cent of the women labourers from the developed villages and 59.2 per cent of the women labourers from the underdeveloped villages contributed 25 to 49 per cent of their family income. This shows that the women labourers in the underdeveloped villages are more conscientious and responsible in sharing the economic burden of their families and hence they even go to far-off places to earn more.

Expenditure on Food

The pattern of family expenditure indicates the family's economic status. Most of the rural labourers (both farm and non-farm labourers) are forced to do manual labour for survival. They spend a high proportion of their earnings for food. In other words, the propensity to consume is high among the rural families, especially the rural poor.

Table 5.18 shows the percentage of expenditure on food: 64.4 per cent of the total respondents stated to be spending 50-74 per cent of their expenditure on food; another 26 per cent reported that the proportion of food expenses came to 75 to 100 per cent; the remaining 9.6 per cent reported that their food expense came within 25 to 49 per cent of the total family expenses.

Village-wise, the majority of the women labourers (70.2 per cent from Chatrapatti, 60.4 per cent from Kiriyampatti, 69.8 per cent from Kathiriyankulam and 63.3 per cent from S.Vadipatti) spent 50 to 74 per cent of their expenditure on food while 29.2 per cent of the women labourers from Indirapuram (an

Table 5.18. Percentage of Expenditure of Food

Block	*Village*	*Expenditure on Food (%)*			
		25-49 %	*50-74 %*	*75-100 %*	*Total %*
	Developed				
Athoor	1. Athoor	12 (7.9)	98 (64.5)	42 (27.6)	152
R.Chatram	2. S.Vadipatti	5 (5.5)	57 (63.3)	28 (31.2)	90
Dindigul	3. Chatrapatti	7 (10.4)	47 (70.2)	13 (19.4)	67
	Total (A)	24 (7.8)	202 (65.4)	83 (26.8)	309 (61.8)
	Underdeveloped				
Athoor	1. Indirapuram	8 (12.3)	38 (58.5)	19 (29.2)	65
R.Chatram	2. Kathiriyankulam	8 (12.7)	44 (69.8)	11 (17.5)	63
Dindigul	3. Kiriyampatti	8 (12.6)	38 (60.4)	17 (27.0)	63
	Total (B)	24 (12.6)	120 (62.8)	47 (24.6)	191 (38.2)
	Grand Total (A+B)	48 (9.6)	322 (64.4)	130 (26.0)	500 (100.0)

Source: Computed from primary data

* Figures in parantheses indicate percentages (Multiple responses)

underdeveloped village) spent 75 to 100 per cent of their expenditure on food.

Group-wise, the number of women labourers whose food expenditure was 50-74 per cent and 75-100 per cent is more in underdeveloped villages, viz. 62.8 per cent as against 65.4 per cent and 24.6 per cent as against 26.8 per cent in developed and underdeveloped villages respectively.

The percentage of expenditure on food spent by 60 per cent of the respondent families was between 50-74. This means that three-fourths of the family expenditure was on food, resulting in deficit of money for other expenses and there could be no saving. This probably forced them even to borrow.

(ii) Problems Related to in their Work Environment

Nature of Work

Usually the wage labourers have to work in any place wherever they get employment opportunities. They may have to work both within their native village as well as outside their village. Table 5.19 shows the types of work available within the village and outside the village of the women labourers. The women labourers of the study were enquired about their usual place of work. To this, the majority of them (93.0 per cent) stated that they generally worked only within their village and the remaining 7.0 per cent stated that they worked anywhere both within and outside the village area.

With regard to the nature of work they were involved in village, 89.8 per cent were engaged in agriculture and allied activities, followed by 7.4 per cent as construction workers. There were 1.6 per cent working in bricks kiln work and 1.2 per cent in the mills (paper board and coir industry).

Those who used to work outside the village reported that their work outside the village included agriculture (74.3 per cent), construction (8.6 per cent) and brick kiln work chamber (17.1 per cent)

Table 5.19. Types of Work Within the Village and Outside the Village

Block	Village	Total	Work within the village				Work outside the village			
			1	2	3	4	5	6	7	Total
	Developed									
Athoor	1. Athoor	152	134 (88.2)	17 (11.1)	1 (0.6)	---	4 (66.6)	1 (16.7)	1 (16.7)	6
R.Chatram	2. S.Vadipatti	90	89 (98.9)	1 (1.1)	---	---	1	---	---	1
Dindigul	3. Chatrapatti	67	57 (85.0)	3 (4.5)	4 (6.0)	3 (4.5)	6 (46.2)	2 (15.4)	5 (38.4)	13
Total (A)		309 (61.8)	280 (90.6)	21 (6.8)	5 (1.6)	3 (1.0)	11 (55.0)	3 (15.0)	6 (30.0)	20 (57.1)
	Underdeveloped									
Athoor	1. Indirapuram	65	65 (100.0)	---	---	---	---	---	---	---
R.Chatram	2. Kathiriyankulam	63	61 (96.8)	2 (3.2)	---	---	5 (100.0)	---	---	5
Dindigul	3. Kiriyampatti	63	43 (68.2)	14 (22.2)	3 (4.8)	3 (4.8)	10 (100.0)	---	---	10
	Total (B)	191 (38.2)	169 (88.4)	16 (8.4)	3 (1.6)	3 (1.6)	15 (100.0)	---	---	15 (42.9)
	Grand Total (A+B)	500 (100.0)	449 (89.8)	37 (7.4)	8 (1.6)	6 (1.2)	26 (74.3)	3 (8.6)	6 (17.1)	35 (7.0)

Source: Computed from primary data * Figures in parantheses indicate percentages(Multiple responses)

1. Agriculture, 2. Construction, 3. Chamber brick works, 4. Mill, 5. Agriculture, 6. Construction, 7. Chamber brick works.

There is no difference in the nature of the work carried out by the women labourers within the village belonging to both category of villages, but, as for the work outside the villages, all the 15 respondents (100 per cent) from the underdeveloped villages, and only 55 per cent of these from the developed villages were involved in agriculture. All those involved in construction and brick kiln work were only from the developed villages. The freedom to move about to any place to work for the women workers is a good sign of getting equal social status. But, in this study, only seven per cent of the women labourers were free to go about to any place to work, whereas the majority (93 per cent) have as their place of work only their native village, which shows that they are not free to choose their area of work and this curtails both their social movement and economic freedom/ development.

It is concluded that agricultural and allied activities are the major type of work of the majority of the women workers both within and outside the village area.

Mode of Transportaion

With regard to mode of transport the women labourers use to reach the workplace, it was observed that they did not use any particular mode of transport. They chose to go to their workspot using various modes depending upon the situation, time and distance; they went on foot to work locally; they also used cycles, public transport facilities, and sometimes, they used the employers' transport facilities. Table 5.20 reveals the mode of reaching the workspot by the women labourers.

Generally, as per their statement, 94.6 per cent of the labourers used to go on foot to their workspot. Whenever they had to go to distant places, they used public transport facilities (23.2 per cent), while 2.8 per cent used cycles and another 2.8 per cent other transport facilities.

Comparatively, almost equal number of women labourers (94.2 per cent) from the developed villages used to walk as from

Table 5.20. Mode of Reaching the Workspot/Home by Women Labourers

Block	*Village*	*No.of Respondents*	*By Foot*	*Cycle*	*Public Transport*	*Employer Transport*
	Developed					
Athoor	1. Athoor	152	150 (98.7)	1 (0.6)	24 (15.8)	3 (2.0)
R.Chatram	2. S.Vadipatti	90	90 (100.0)	1 (1.1)	10 (11.1)	---
Dindigul	3. Chatrapatti	67	51 (76.1)	1 (1.4)	21 (31.3)	3 (4.4)
Total (A)		309 (61.8)	291 (94.2)	3 (1.0)	55 (17.9)	6 (1.9)
	Underdeveloped					
Athoor	1. Indirapuram	65	65 (100.0)	---	22 (33.8)	1 (1.5)
R.Chatram	2. Kathiriyankulam	63	63 (100.0)	9 (14.2)	24 (38.1)	6 (9.5)
Dindigul	3. Kiriyampatti	63	54 (85.7)	2 (3.1)	15 (23.8)	1 (1.5)
	Total (B)	191 (38.2)	182 (95.3)	11 (5.8)	61 (31.9)	8 (4.2)
	Grand Total (A+B)	500 (100.0)	473 (94.6)	14 (2.8)	116 (23.2)	14 (2.8)

Source: Computed from primary data

* Figures in parantheses indicate percentages(Multiple responses)

the underdeveloped villages (94.6 per cent). But the use of cycle is more among the women labourers of underdeveloped villages (5.8 per cent) than from the developed villages (1.0 per cent), while 31.9 per cent of the respondents from the underdeveloped villages used public transport facilities as compared to 17.9 from the developed villages. Walking was the mode of reaching the workplace by 94.6 per cent of the respondents.

The use of public transport facilities (31.9 per cent) is more by the respondents from the underdeveloped villages as compared to 17.9 per cent from the developed villages since they have to go a long distance to work in the mills.

Reasons for the Choice of Labour and Employment Position

The need for women's employment is felt in our country. Assured employment gives economic status to women. Gender disparity reduces the participation of women not only in employment but also in the process of economic development. Women's work is less paid, less valued, and recognition to women's work is also poor. Women participation in labour force not only depends upon the prevailing employment opportunities, but also depends upon the material and ideological constraints women face in the society. Table 5.21 shows the women labourers' reasons for choosing their employment.

Several factors, physical, technical, economic and social, determine the availability of employment. Any change in these factors may affect the employment situation. In India 70 per cent of the people depend upon agriculture as their main source of employment. Due to absence of non-farm activities in the rural areas, people are forced to take up agriculture as their main source of livelihood. The women labourers of the study explained the reasons for choosing their present employment. The major reason was the non-availability of other work, as expressed by 60.6 per cent of the women labourers; availability of employment within the village helped a lot to the labourers, especially women

Table 5.21. Reason for choosing their Occupation among Women Labourers

Block	*Village*	*1*	*2*	*3*	*4*	*5*	*6*	*7*	*Total*
	Developed								
Athoor	1. Athoor	81 (53.3)	73 (48.6)	21 (13.8)	9 (5.4)	---	2 (1.3)	---	152
R.Chatram	2.S.Vadipatti	46 (51.1)	53 (58.8)	21 (23.3)	---	1 (1.1)	2 (2.2)	13 (14.4)	90
Dindigul	3.Chatrapatti	44 (65.7)	38 (56.7)	5 (7.5)	12 (17.9)	4 (5.9)	2 (3.0)	---	67
Total (A)		171 (55.3)	164 (53.1)	47 (15.2)	21 (5.5)	5 (1.6)	6 (1.9)	13 (4.2)	309 (61.8)
	Underdeveloped								
Athoor	1.Indirapuram	37 (70.8)	37 (70.8)	30 (46.1)	---	---	---	---	65
R.Chatram	2.Kathiriyankulam	28 (44.4)	45 (71.4)	42 (66.7)	---	---	---	---	63
Dindigul	3.Kiriyampatti	39 (61.9)	57 (90.5)	10 (15.9)	2 (3.2)	1 (1.6)	---	---	63
	Total (B)	104 (54.4)	139 (72.8)	82 (42.9)	2 (1.0)	1 (0.5)	---	---	191 (38.2)
	Grand Total (A+B)	275 (55.0)	303 (60.6)	129 (25.8)	23 (4.6)	6 (1.2)	6 (1.2)	13 (2.6)	500 (100.0)

Source: Computed from primary data * Figures in parantheses indicate percentages (Multiple responses)

1. Availability of work within the village; 2. Non-availability of other work; 3. No other skill; 4. Get better wage; 5. Get regular employment; 6 Manual work without skill; 7. Run the family

labourers and this became the reason for 55.0 per cent of the women labourers for choosing their occupation 25.8 per cent of the women labourers expressed that they did not possess other skills and hence they fell in the present occupation. Getting a better wage rate was the reason for 4.6 per cent of the women labourers; getting regular employment in the opinion of another 1.2 per cent of the women labourers, was the reason; and, the remaining 2.6 per cent stated that they chosen their work just to run their family without any specific justification.

Group-wise, non-availability of any other work was stated by a higher percentage of respondents (72.8 per cent) from the underdeveloped villages than from the developed villages (53.1 per cent). More number of respondents (42.9 per cent) from the underdeveloped villages stated that they had no other skills while the same reason was attributed only by 15.2 per cent of the respondents from the developed villages. Getting regular employment was stated as a reason by 1.6 per cent of the respondents in the developed villages and by 0.5 per cent from the underdeveloped villages.

Non-availability any other work (60.6 per cent), and availability of work within the village (55 per cent) were the major reasons by the respondents to choose their present occupation. This shows that they do not want to depend only upon agricultural labour, but, as they have to find some employment opportunities to support their family income they are left with no other alternative to choose any other employment. If they are given any training in rural-based employment opportunities in other trades, probably they may shift from the present occupation. The rural landless labourers do not have continuous work. The majority of the landless labourers (especially the women labourers) depend on agriculture for their source of livelihood. As agriculture is a seasonal occupation, on an average, a farm labourer finds employment for about 200 days in a year and for the rest of the year is idle. The problem of unemployment and underemployment is still increasing because of lack of non-agricultural occupations in the rural areas. Table 5.22 depicts the distribution of women labourers according to their employment position. As mentioned earlier the main occupation of 91.4 per cent of the women labourers is agricultural labour and the remaining 8.6 per cent are labourers in the non-agricultural sector. Among those involved as agricultural labour, more than three-fourths (78.8 per cent) get employment chances for 10-20 days per month, while another 14.0 per cent go for work for less than 10 days in a month. The period of employment is somewhere between 21-30 days in a month in the case of 7.2 per cent of the women labourers. Among the non-agricultural labourers, 60.5 per cent have reported to work for 10-20 days in a month, whereas the employment chances are less than 10 days in a month in the case of 23.3 per cent of these women labourers. The highest range of 21-30 days has been reported by 16.2 per cent of the non-agricultural labourers.

In the case of subsidiary occupation, among the agricultural labourers 80.2 per cent and 67.6 per cent of the non-agricultural labourers get work for only less than 10 days in a month. A little above one-fourth of the non-agricultural labourers (26.5 per cent) and 79.9 per cent of the agriculture labourers have reported to get work for 10-20 days in a month. The highest number of 21-30 days in a month has been reported only by the non- agricult ural labourers (5.9 per cent). All the agricultural labourers from the developed villages and 80.9 per cent of the non-agricultural labourers from the underdeveloped villages were employed for only less than 10 days in a month.

As for the main occupation, the majority of the agricultural labourers (78.8 per cent) and 60.5 per cent of the non-agricultural labourers reported to work for 10-20 days in a month.

The majority of the agricultural labourers (84.6 per cent) from the underdeveloped villages and 71.4 per cent of the non-agricultural labourers from the developed villages got employment for 10-20 days in a month. This shows that in the developed

Table 5.22 : Employment Position of Women Labourers

Block	Village	Main								Total
		Agriculture				Non - Agriculture				
		Below 10	10 - 20	21 - 30	Total	Below 10	10 - 20	21 - 30	Total	
	Developed									
Athoor	1. Athoor	22 (15.2)	114 (78.6)	9 (6.2)	145 (95.4)	5 (71.4)	2 (28.6)	---	7 (4.6)	152
R.Chatram	2. S.Vadipatti	12 (13.8)	69 (79.3)	6 (6.9)	87 (96.7)	1 (33.3)	2 (66.7)	---	3 (3.3)	90
Dindigul	3. Chatrapatti	16 (28.6)	34 (60.7)	6 (10.7)	56 (83.6)	---	11 (100.0)	---	11 (16.4)	67
Total (A)		50 (17.4)	217 (75.3)	21 (7.3)	288 (93.2)	6 (28.6)	15 (71.4)	---	21 (6.8)	309 (61.8)
	Underdeveloped									
Athoor	1. Indirapuram	3 (4.6)	57 (87.7)	5 (7.7)	65 (100.0)	---	---	---	---	65
R.Chatram	2. Kathiriyankulam	2 (3.3)	54 (90.0)	4 (6.7)	60 (95.2)	---	3 (100.0)	---	3 (4.8)	63
Dindigul	3. Kiriyampatti	9 (20.5)	32 (72.7)	3 (6.8)	44 (69.8)	4 (21.1)	8 (42.1)	7 (36.8)	19 (30.1)	63
	Total (B)	14 (8.3)	143 (84.6)	12 (7.1)	169 (88.5)	4 (18.2)	11 (50.0)	7 (31.8)	22 (11.5)	191 (38.2)
	Grand Total (A+B)	64 (14.0)	360 (78.8)	33 (7.2)	457 (91.4)	10 (23.3)	26 (60.5)	7 (16.2)	43 (8.6)	500

Block	Village	Subsidary								Total
		Agriculture				Non - Agriculture				
		Below 10	10 - 20	21 - 30	Total	Below 10	10 - 20	21 - 30	Total	
	Developed									
Athoor	1. Athoor	4 (100.0)	---	---	4 (28.6)	6 (60.0)	4 (40.0)	---	10 (71.4)	14 (9.2)
R.Chatram	2. S.Vadipatti	1 (100.0)	---	---	1 (100.0)	---	---	---	---	1 (1.1)
Dindigul	3. Chatrapatti	10 (100.0)	---	---	10 (76.9)	---	2 (66.7)	1 (33.3)	3 (23.1)	13 (19.4)
	Total (A)	15 (100.0)	---	---	15 (53.6)	6 (46.2)	6 (46.2)	1 (7.6)	13 (46.4)	28 (45.2)
	Underdeveloped									
Athoor	1. Indirapuram	---	---	---	---	3 (100.0)	---	---	3 (100.0)	3 (4.6)
R.Chatram	2. Kathiriyankulam	3 (100.0)	---	---	3 (27.3)	5 (62.5)	3 (37.5)	---	8 (77.7)	11 (17.5)
Dindigul	3. Kiriyampatti	5 (50.0)	5 (50.0)	---	10 (50.0)	9 (90.0)	---	1 (10.0)	10 (50.0)	20 (31.7)
	Total (B)	8 (61.6)	5 (38.4)	---	13 (38.2)	17 (80.9)	3 (14.3)	1 (4.8)	21 (61.8)	34 (54.8)
	Grand Total (A+B)	23 (82.1)	5 (17.9)	---	28 (45.2)	23 (67.6)	9 (26.5)	2 (5.9)	34 (54.8)	62 (12.4)

Source: Computed from primary data

* Figures in parantheses indicate percentages (Multiple responses)

villages the labourers do not depend mainly on agriculture. Instead, they go out for other work. In case of subsidiary occupations, 82.1 per cent of the agricultural and 67.6 per cent of the non-agricultural labourers got work for less than 10 days in a month.

Unemployment

Unemployment has been defined as a situation when a person who is able and willing to work does not get a suitable employment opportunity and hence he is denied access to a source of income. The nature of unemployment in the rural sector differs, from that in the urban sector-generally, in the rural sector, two types of unemployment exist viz. seasonal unemployment and disguished unemployment. It is well a known fact that unemployment in the agricultural sector is seasonal and the marginal productivity of additional labour employed in the agricultural sector is equal to zero. In other words the employment of additional labour does not contribute any thing to the total output. Table 5.23 indicates the various reasons for unemployment stated by the women labourers.

When the women labourers were enquired about the reasons for unemployment, they attributed five types of reasons and they are poor rainfall (75.2 per cent), poor employment opportunities (62.2 per cent), seasonal occupation (22.0 per cent), lack of raw materials (4.4 per cent) and population growth (1.0 per cent).

Category-wise, 80.2 per cent of the women labourers from the underdeveloped villages and 70.9 per cent of those from the developed villages stated poor rainfall as the main reason for unemployment. More number of women labourers (67.0 per cent) from the developed villages cited poor employment opportunities, whereas the same reason was reported only by 59.2 per cent from the developed villages. Seasonal occupation was attributed by the women labourers from underdeveloped villages (23.0 per cent) and by those from developed villages (21.3 per cent). More

Table 5.23. Reasons for Unemployment among Women Labourers

Block	Village	Total	Reasons for unemployment *				
			1	2	3	4	5
	Developed						
Athoor	1. Athoor	152	90 (59.2)	104 (68.4)	24 (15.8)	18 (11.8)	4 (2.0)
R.Chatram	2.S.Vadipatti	90	83 (92.2)	59 (65.6)	32 (35.6)	---	---
Dindigul	3.Chattapatti	67	46 (68.7)	20 (29.8)	10 (14.9)	3 (4.5)	1 (1.4)
	Total (A)	309 (61.8)	219 (70.9)	183 (59.2)	66 (21.3)	21 (6.8)	5 (1.6)
	Underdeveloped						
Athoor	1. Indirapuram	65	56 (86.1)	29 (44.6)	7 (10.8)	---	1 (1.5)
R.Chatram	2. Kathiriyankulam	63	40 (63.5)	49 (77.8)	25 (39.7)	---	---
Dindigul	3. Kiriyampatti	63	61 (96.7)	50 (79.4)	12 (19.0)	1 (1.5)	---
	Total (B)	191 (38.2)	157 (82.2)	128 (67.0)	44 (23.0)	1 (0.5)	---
	Grand Total (A+B)	500 (100.0)	376 (75.2)	311 (62.2)	110 (22.0)	22 (4.4)	5 (1.0)

Source: Computed from primary data * Figures in parantheses indicate percentages (Multiple responses)

1. Poor rainfall, 2. Poor employment opportunities, 3. Seasonal occupation, 4. Lack of of rainfall, 5. Population growth

number of women labourers (6.8 per cent) from developed villages reported lack of raw materials in the industries (coir, brick kiln and paper board) as reason for unemployment and the same reason was been attributed by 0.5 per cent of the women labourers from the underdeveloped villages. Poor rainfall (75.2 per cent), poor employment opportunities (62 per cent), seasonal occupation (22 per cent) are the major reasons for unemployment among the study women labourers.

Group-wise, only 70.9 per cent of those from the developed villages have expressed poor rainfall because these villages have better irrigation facilities than the underdeveloped villages with only rainfed area, and hence a higher percentage (82.2 per cent) of them have attributed poor rainfall as a major reason for unemployment in their villages. In order to improve the employment situation in the study region, the governmental agencies should formulate and design micro level employment module which should suit the local needs and aspirations. The module should aim at increasing the area under cultivation by providing proper irrigation facility through construction of percolation pond, and promote waterharvesting system during rainy seasons. Further it should have an objective to provide training to rural women in non-farm activities, which promote employment generation during off-season.

Gender Discrimination in Wage

In India, although the Minimum Wages Act was passed in 1948, followed subsequently by the Equal Remuneration Act in 1976, obtaining minimum wages or equal remuneration is still a far cry, particularly in the case of workers working in the unorganised sector of the country. Wage differentials in terms of the legal minimum and gender are also common. The wage rates prevailing in the study villages have been presented in the Table 5.24. The maximum amount of wage given is Rs.60 and in the case of Athoor and Chatrapatti villages, the maximum wage is Rs. 80 per day. For females the highest amount of Rs.55, paid in

Chatrapatti village and in Athoor and Kathirayankulam villages. The lowest wage rate of Rs. 20 has been reported by the respondents. As for the wage rate for men workers 89.8 per cent of them stated Rs. 26-50 per day while another 9.2 per cent of them revealed it to be Rs. 51-75 per day in their villages. For women, the wage rate was Rs. 25 per day as reported by 92.0 per cent of the women labourers.

A comparative analysis shows that the wage rate of Rs. 26 to Rs. 50 has been stated by more than 90.9 per cent of the men labourers of developed villages and 88.0 per cent of men of underdeveloped villages. But in the case of women 82.7 per cent of women labourers from underdeveloped villages have reported upto Rs. 25 as against 97.7 per cent of them in the developed villages. On the contrary, a higher percentage of women labourers (17.3 per cent) from the underdeveloped villages (as against 1.1 per cent from the developed villages) have reported a higher wage rate of 26-50 per day.

In the study villages, the male gets Rs.26-90 per day as his wage depending upon the nature of his work, as was stated by 90 per cent of the respondents.

Group-wise, the female gets Rs.26-50 as reported by 17.3 per cent of the respondents from the underdeveloped village because of their non-agricultural sector work and only 1 per cent of them from the developed villages reported this rate.

The labour market in India is characterised by wide differences in the level of wages across status and even across regions within a state; labourers expect wages depending on the nature of their employment and their levels of skill; those workers having a higher capacity and skill expect higher wages. Table 5.25 shows the reported reasons for wage difference among men and women labourers.

The wages are not paid equally to both men and women labourers. There are differences of wage between these two. The women labourers were asked to spell out the reasons for such

Table 5.24. Prevailing Wages (in Rs)

Block	Village	Male				Female		
		26-50	51-75	75+	Total	Upto 25	26-50	51-75
	Developed							
Athoor	1. Athoor	145 (95.4)	4 (2.6)	3 (2.0)	152	152 (100.0)	---	---
R.Chatram	2. S.Vadipatti	89 (98.9)	1 (1.1)	---	90	90 (100.0)	---	---
Dindigul	3. Chatrapatti	47 (70.1)	18 (26.9)	2 (3.0)	67	60 (89.5)	3 (4.4)	4 (5.9)
Total (A)		281 (90.9)	23 (7.5)	5 (1.6)	309 (61.8)	302 (97.7)	3 (1.0)	4 (1.3)
	Underdeveloped							
Athoor	1.Indirapuram	65 (100.0)	---	---	65	65 (100.0)	---	---
R.Chatram	2.Kathiriyankulam	48 (76.2)	15 (23.8)	---	63	48 (76.1)	15 (23.8)	---
Dindigul	3.Kiriyampatti	55 (87.3)	8 (12.6)	---	63	45 (71.4)	18 (28.6)	---
	Total (B)	168 (88.0)	23 (12.0)	---	191 (38.2)	158 (82.7)	33 (17.3)	---
	Grand Total (A+B)	449 (89.8)	46 (9.2)	5 (1.0)	500 (100.0)	460 (92.0)	36 (7.2)	4 (0.8)

Source: Computed from primary data

* Figures in parantheses indicate percentages (Multiple responses)

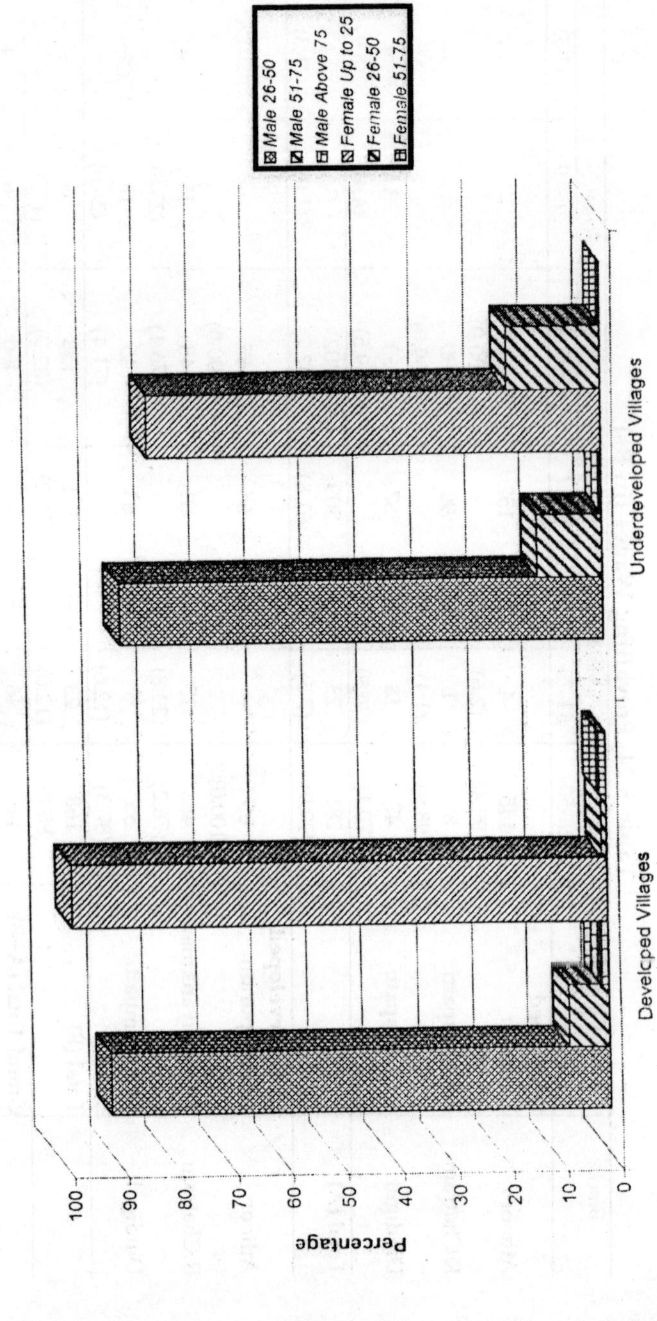

Figure IV
Prevailing Wages (in Rs)

Table 5.25. Reasons for Wage Difference among Men and Women Labourers.

Block	*Village*	*1*	*2*	*3*	*4*	*Total*
	Developed					
Athoor	1. Athoor	94 (61.8)	12 (7.9)	3 (1.9)	55 (36.2)	152
R.Chatram	2. S.Vadipatti	85 (94.4)	24 (26.7)	---	---	90
Dindigul	3. Chatrapatti	64 (95.5)	13 (19.4)	1 (1.4)	1 (1.4)	67
Total (A)		243 (78.6)	49 (15.8)	4 (1.3)	56 (18.1)	309 (61.8)
	Underdeveloped					
Athoor	1. Indirapuram	60 (92.3)	1 (1.5)	1 (1.5)	4 (6.1)	65
R.Chatram	2. Kathiriyankulam	61 (96.8)	14 (22.2)	---	---	63
Dindigul	3. Kiriyampatti	61 (96.8)	26 (41.3)	1 (1.5)	1 (1.5)	63
	Total (B)	182 (95.3)	41 (21.5)	2 (11.0)	5 (12.6)	191 (38.2)
	Grand Total (A+B)	425 (85.0)	90 (18.0)	6 (1.2)	61 (12.2)	500 (100.0)

Source: Computed from primary data * Figures in parantheses indicate percentages (Multiple responses)

1. Male able to do all work, 2. Traditional way followed, 3. Additional skill, 4- Hardship in work

differences in the wage structure. They atributed three reasons: (i) men alone are able to do all types of work and hence they are given higher wages, which was stated by 85 per cent of the respondents, (ii) another 18.0 per cent stated that this system of higher wage rate for men was being followed traditionally: and (iii) the remaining 12.2 per cent said that some work need hard work and only men can do them, (Gender wage differentials were caused by differences in skill, while discriminatory differentials emerged from unequal returns to equal skills. Indian women were endowed with less favourable wage generating characteristics than men-Usha:1983). Comparatively, the reason that men can do all work was spelt out by more women labourers (95.3 per cent) in the underdeveloped villages than from the developed villages (78.6 per cent). Similarly, 21.5 per cent of these from underdeveloped villages and 15.8 per cent of these from the developed villages stated that this system is being followed traditionally. But the need for more money for hard work by men has been emphasized by more women labourers (18.1 per cent) from the developed villages than from the underdeveloped villages (2.6 per cent).

In the view of the majority of the respondents (85 per cent) the males can do all types of work and so they are given a higher wage than females. Equal work and equal pay concept must be practised by the employer so that we can promote and practice human rights and empowerment to rural women. Practising this kind of ethics in the workplace can promote productivity and efficiency among the women labourers.

Nature of Wage and Anomalies in Payment

The nature of payment of wages in the study villages is presented in Table 5.26. It is observed from the table that 83.8 per cent of the women labourers reported receiving their wages daily whereas 15.8 per cent got their wages once in a week. The wages are paid once in a month to 0.4 per cent of the women labourers.

Figure V

Reasons for Wage Difference among Men and Women Labourers

Table 5.26. Nature of Wage Payments

Block	*Village*	*Daily*	*Weekly*	*Monthly*	*Total*
	Developed				
Athoor	1. Athoor	151 (93.3)	1 (0.7)	---	152
R.Chatram	2. S.Vadipatti	84 (93.3)	6 (6.7)	---	90
Dindigul	3. Chatrapatti	36 (53.7)	29 (43.3)	2 (3.0)	67
	Total (A)	271 (87.7)	36 (11.6)	2 (0.7)	309 (61.8)
	Underdeveloped				
Athoor	1.Indirapuram	65 (100.0)	---	---	65
R.Chatram	2.Kathiriyankulam	58 (92.1)	5 (7.9)	---	63
Dindigul	3.Kiriyampatti	25 (38.5)	38 (58.5)	---	63
	Total (B)	148 (77.5)	43 (22.5)	---	191 (38.2)
	Grand Total (A+B)	419 (83.8)	79 (15.8)	2 (0.4)	500 (100.0)

Source: Computed from primary data * Figures in parantheses indicate percentages (Multiple responses)

The respondents who get their wages daily are more (87.7 per cent) in the developed villages than from the underdeveloped villages (77.5 per cent). But more number of women labourers (22.5 per cent) from the underdeveloped villages receive their wages weekly as compared to their counterparts (11.6 per cent) in the developed villages. The two women labourers who get monthly wages are from the developed villages. Daily payment of wage is the nature in case of the majority of the respondents (83.8 per cent).

Group-wise, 87.7 per cent from the developed villages and 77.5 per cent from the underdeveloped villages get daily wages. More number of respondents (22.5 per cent) from the underdeveloped villages get their wages weekly once, because the women labourers from the underdeveloped villages used to work mainly in mills (non-agricultural sector). It is observed from the field that the majority of the women labourers receive daily wage and this is evidence of temporary employment. Moreover wages are paid only in cash and not in kind. Even if the employer is ready to give wage in kind, the women labourers want to have wage in terms of money. Hence monetisation of work is a practice among the women labourers.

In rural areas women labourers are invariably paid much less than men workers. On full time basis they are involve in work in such areas as beedi-making, coir industries, building construction and plantation work, etc. It is stated by the women labourers that employers exploit the women labourers in distributing the wages. Table 5.27 depicts the various types of exploitation in getting wages by the women labourers.

It is noticed from the table that 29.4 per cent of the women labourers reported that they face problem in getting their wages after work. The remaining 70.6 per cent did not face any problem. The major types of problems expressed by them include overtime work without any additional wages (54.5 per cent), delay in payment of wage (22.7 per cent), having to wait for a longer time to receive wages (10.3 per cent) and the demand for commission by the agents and contractors (10.3 per cent).

Table 5.27. Exploitation of Women Labourers in Getting their Wage

Block	Village	Exploitation		Type of Exploitation *			
		Yes	No	1	2	3	4
	Developed						
Athoor	1. Athoor	44 (28.9)	108 (71.1)	38 (86.4)	1 (2.3)	---	5 (11.3)
R.Chatram	2. S.Vadipatti	22 (24.4)	68 (75.6)	5 (22.7)	10 (45.4)	7 (31.8)	---
Dindigul	3. Chatrapatti	27 (40.3)	40 (59.7)	14 (51.8)	7 (25.9)	3 (11.1)	2 (7.4)
Total (A)		93 (30.1)	216 (69.9)	57 (61.3)	18 (19.3)	10 (10.7)	7 (7.5)
	Underdeveloped						
Athoor	1. Indirapuram	15 (23.0)	50 (77.0)	11 (73.3)	4 (26.7)	---	---
R.Chatram	2. Kathiriyankulam	15 (23.8)	48 (76.1)	2 (13.3)	11 (73.3)	---	2 (13.3)
Dindigul	3. Kiriyampatti	24 (38.0)	39 (62.0)	9 (37.5)	5 (20.8)	5 (20.8)	6 (25.0)
	Total (B)	54 (28.3)	137 (71.7)	22 (40.7)	15 (27.8)	5 (9.2)	8 (14.8)
	Grand Total (A+B)	147 (29.4)	353 (70.6)	79 (54.5)	33 (22.7)	15 (10.3)	15 (10.3)

Source: Computed from primary data * Figures in parantheses indicate percentages (Multiple responses)

1. Overtime work without wage 2. Delay in payment 3. Waiting for a longer time to receive wage 4. Commission to contractors/agents

Figure VI
Exploitation of Women Labourers In Getting their Wage

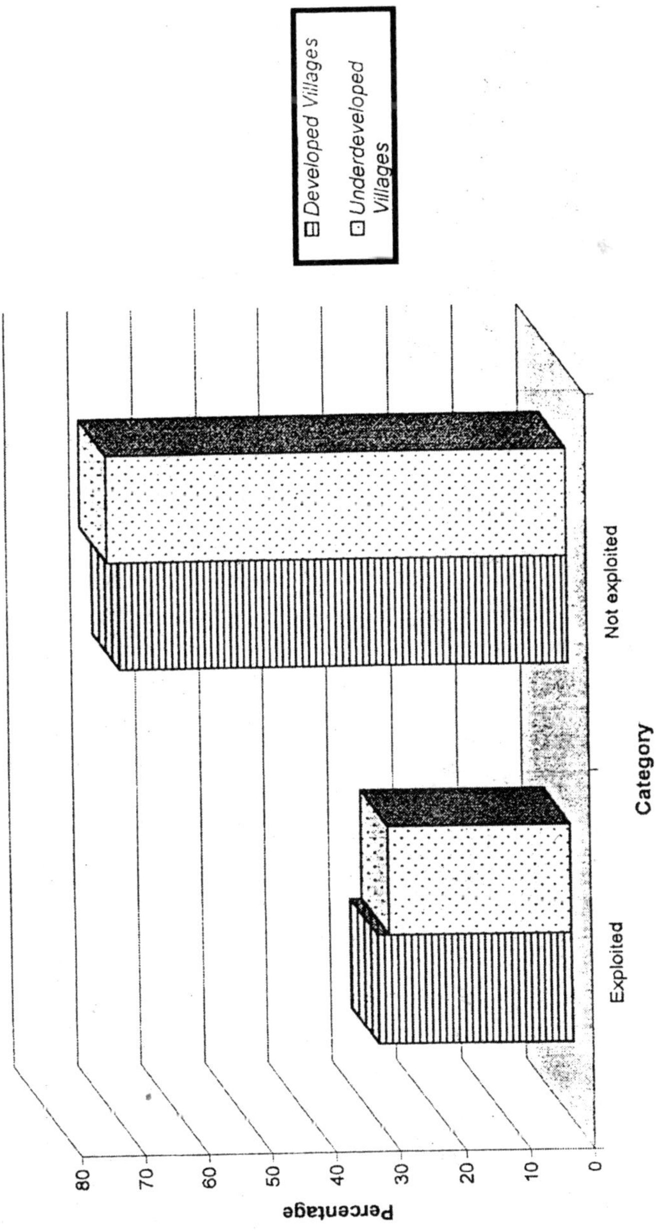

Group-wise, 30.1 per cent of the labourers from the developed villages and 28.3 per cent from the underdeveloped villages have reported the above-cited problems. These types of problems are present in both the type of villages.

Work Environment and Wage Distribution

It is a general understanding that the workers should be provided with some basic facilities and this will motivate them to good work. But the women labourers of this study, being only rural workers in the unorganised sector, do not seem to enjoy any such facility. Table 5.28 shows the facilities available to the women labourers at the workspot. Out of the 500 women labourers, only 11 per cent have stated that they enjoy some facility while the facilities are not available to the remaining majority (89 per cent) of them.

With regard to the type of facility, half of the women labourers (50.9 per cent) enjoying facilities have reported that there are balwadies, while one-fourth (25.4 per cent) have first aid facility. The other types of facilities available include rest room (18.1 per cent), toilet (14.5 per cent), canteen (12.7 per cent) and creche (10.9 per cent).

More number of women labourers from the developed villages have reported to have canteen facility (15.1 per cent), rest room facility (27.3 per cent), and, creche facility (12.1 per cent). On the other hand the women labourers from underdeveloped villages reported to have balwadies (54.5 per cent) and facilities for first aid (31.8 per cent).

Only 11 per cent of the women labourers expressed that they enjoy some facilities like day care centre, first aid facilities, rest room, toilet, canteen and creche in their workspot.

The above analysis shows that the workers in the unorganised sector need to be given a number of basic facilities. The women labourers in the rural areas are unaware of the standard working hours for their work. This may be due to illiteracy and lack of unionisation in the study areas.

Table 5.28. Facilities Available for Women Labourers at Workplace

Block	*Village*	*Facilities*		*Types of Facilities **					
		Available	*Not available*	*Creche*	*Balwadi*	*Toilet*	*Canteen*	*Rest room*	*First aid*
	Developed								
Athoor	1. Athoor	4 (2.6)	148 (97.4)	---	---	1 (25.0)	1 (25.0)	1 (25.0)	1 (25.0)
R.Chatram	2. S.Vadipatti	12 (13.3)	78 (86.7)	---	12 (100.0)	---	---	---	---
Dindigul	3. Chatrapatti	17 (25.3)	50 (74.6)	4 (23.5)	4 (23.5)	4 (23.5)	4 (23.5)	8 (47.0)	6 (35.3)
Total (A)		33 (10.7)	276 (89.3)	4 (12.1)	16 (48.5)	5 (15.1)	5 (15.1)	9 (27.3)	7 (21.2)
	Underdeveloped								
Athoor	1. Indirapuram	10 (15.4)	55 (84.6)	---	10 (100.0)	1 (10.0)	1 (10.0)	---	---
R.Chatram	2. Kathiriyankulam	---	63 (100.0)	---	---	---	---	---	---
Dindigul	3. Kiriyampatti	12 (19.0)	51 (81.0)	2 (16.7)	2 (16.7)	2 (16.7)	1 (8.3)	1 (8.3)	7 (58.3)
	Total (B)	22 (11.5)	169 (88.5)	2 (9.1)	12 (54.5)	3 (13.6)	2 (9.1)	1 (4.5)	7 (31.8)
	Grand Total (A+B)	55 (11.0)	445 (89.0)	6 (10.9)	28 (50.9)	8 (14.5)	7 (12.7)	10 (18.1)	14 (25.4)

Source: Computed from primary data

* Figures in parantheses indicate percentages (Multiple responses)

Table 5.29 reveals that 90.8 per cent of the women labourers were not aware of the standard working hours while the remaining 9.2 per cent were aware of the fixed working hours.

More than 90.0 per cent of the women labourers from both the category of villages were not aware of it. The awareness was nil in case of 91.6 per cent of the respondents in the underdeveloped villages whereas 90.3 per cent of those from the developed villages were not aware of it.

Among those who were aware of the fixed working hours, more (9.7 per cent) were from the developed villages. As for the maximum hours they work, among the women labourers of the developed villages, 60.5 per cent have reported to work for 7-8 hours a day whereas another 23.0 per cent work for 8-10 hours a day. Some women labourers (11 per cent) revealed that they had to work for more than 10 hours a day.

Among the women labourers of underdeveloped villages, 64.4 per cent used to work for 7-8 hours a day followed by 14.6 per cent who work for 8-10 hours. The maximum duration of working time of 10 hours and above was reported by 21.0 per cent of women labourers.

The majority of the women labourers (90.8 per cent) expressed ignorance about the fixed working hours as per government rule. This may be because of their illiteracy and their negligence to know the rules and also because there is nobody to educate them about this. Also, as this is an unorganised sector, no trade union involvement is seen and this may also be one of the reasons. Efforts must be taken to propagate and make such workers to gain awareness about the government rules with regard to the working hours.

Again, though the majority of the labourers are not aware of the rules of the working hours, 60.5 per cent of them used to work only for 7-8 hours a day which is in accordance with the rules. But the fact that 23.0 per cent of them have to work for more than 8 hours, needs to be looked in to and this may be

Table 5.29. Awareness about Standard Working Hours among Women Labourers

Block	Village	Awareness			Working Hours			
		Yes	No	Total	Below 7	7 - 8	8 - 10	Above 10
	Developed							
Athoor	1. Athoor	7 (4.6)	145 (95.4)	152	15 (9.8)	81 (53.3)	45 (29.6)	11 (7.2)
R.Chatram	2.S.Vadipatti	2 (2.2)	88 (97.8)	90	---	79 (87.8)	8 (8.9)	3 (3.3)
Dindigul	3.Chatrapatti	21 (31.3)	46 (68.7)	67	2 (3.0)	27 (40.2)	18 (26.9)	20 (29.8)
Total (A)		30 (9.7)	279 (90.3)	309 (61.8)	17 (5.5)	187 (60.5)	71 (23.0)	34 (11.0)
	Underdeveloped							
Athoor	1.Indirapuram	4 (6.1)	61 (93.2)	65	---	65 (100.0)	---	---
R.Chatram	2.Kathiriyankulam	---	63 (100.0)	63	---	23 (36.5)	10 (15.9)	30 (47.6)
Dindigul	3.Kiriyampatti	12 (19.0)	51 (81.0)	63	---	25 (39.7)	18 (28.6)	20 (31.7)
	Total (B)	16 (8.4)	175 (91.6)	191 (38.2)	---	123 (64.4)	28 (14.6)	40 (21.0)
	Grand Total (A+B)	46 (9.2)	454 (90.8)	500 (100.0)	17 (3.4)	310 (62.0)	99 (19.8)	74 (14.8)

Source: Computed from primary data

* Figures in parantheses indicate percentages (Multiple responses)

because of their ignorance and hence, the employers try to exploit their labour.

The labourers in the informal sector use to work for more hours than specified and they do not adhere strictly to the rules of working hours for various reasons. Table 5.30 shows the number of days worked more than the specified working hours by the women labourers. Among the 500 respondents of this study, 145 (29.0 per- cent) revealed that they do not strictly watch the hours of work but they generally do work for more hours. Among those who used to work for extra hours, 73.1 per cent of the women labourers reported that they used to work for less than 10 days in a month. The number of days of additional hours of work by 22.7 per cent of them was on 11 to 20 days per month while the remaining 4.2 per cent were involved in overtime work for more than 20 days in a month.

Group-wise, the percentage of respondents working for additional hours is higher (62.1 per cent) from the developed villages than from the underdeveloped villages (37.9 per cent). The number of days of extra work is only less than 10 in the case of a higher per centage of women labourers (85.6 per cent) from the developed villages. On the contrary, 36.4 per cent of the women labourers from the underdeveloped villages work for 11 to 20 days in a month. All the six women labourers involved in additional work for more than 20 days were from underdeveloped villages.

Among these workers who worked extra hours, 51.5 per cent revealed that they were given an incentive of Rs.6 to Rs.10 per day for their extra work, while 45.4 per cent said that they were given only less than Rs. 5 per day as incentive. Two women labourers have received more than Rs.10 per day as incentive for extra work.

Though the incidence of overtime work prevails, it was reported only by 29 per cent of the respondents. Even among such labourers the majority of them (73.1 per cent) do overtime work only for 10 days in a month.

Table 5.30. Number of Days Worked more than Specified Working Hours among Women Labourers

Block	Village	No.of Days				Incentive in (Rs.)				
		Below 10	11-20	Above 20-30	Total	Below 5	6-10	10-15	Above 15	Total
	Developed									
Athoor	1. Athoor	45 (88.2)	6 11.8)	---	51 (33.6)	8 (61.5)	4 (30.8)	---	1 (7.7)	13 (25.5)
R.Chatram	2.S.Vadipatti	3 (50.0)	3 (50.0)	---	6 (6.7)	1 (100.0)	---	---	---	1 (16.7)
Dindigul	3.Chatrapatti	29 (87.9)	4 (12.1)	---	33 (49.2)	11 (57.9)	8 (42.1)	---	---	19 (57.6)
	Total (A)	77 (85.6)	13 (14.4)	---	90 (62.1)	20 (60.6)	12 (36.4)	---	1 (3.0)	33 (50.0)
	Underdeveloped									
Athoor	1.Indirapuram	19 (67.8)	9 (32.8)	---	28 (43.0)	4 (23.5)	13 (76.5)	---	---	17 (60.7)
R.Chatram	2.Kathiriyankulam	2 (100.0)	---	---	2 (3.1)	---	---	---	---	---
Dindigul	3.Kiriyampatti	8 (32.0)	11 (44.0)	6 (24.0)	25 (39.7)	6 (37.5)	9 (56.3)	5 (6.2)	---	16 (64.0)
	Total (B)	29 (52.7)	20 (36.4)	6 (10.9)	55 (37.9)	10 (30.3)	22 (62.7)	1 (3.0)	---	33 (50.0)
	Grand Total (A+B)	106 (73.1)	33 (22.7)	6 (4.2)	145 (29.0)	30 (45.4)	34 (51.5)	1 (1.5)	1 (1.5)	66 (45.5)

Source: Computed from primary data

* Figures in parantheses indicate percentages (Multiple responses)

Among the overtime workers, 51.5 per cent used to get Rs. 6-10 per day for the extra work done, which will help them to meet minor expenses of the family. Efforts should be made by the women labourers to form an organisation so that they can bargain with the employer for obtaining compensation for their extra work. Hence there is a need to form an effective women's labour union which can protect the welfare of the women labourers.

Most workers in India work in the informal sector. The Minimum Wage legislation is the most important labour act for ensuring minimum wages to the workers in this sector. The Minimum Wages Act, 1948, provides for legal action against an employer if he does not pay the minimum wage. Yet, many workers do not get minimum wages. There are several reasons for the poor implementation of minimum wage legislation. Lack of awareness about the minimum wage provisions is a major reason for its ineffectiveness. This is particularly true in remote areas and in areas where there is no organisation for labourers.

Details regarding the women labourers' awareness about the Minimum Wage Act have been presented in Table 5.31. Out of the 500 sample women labourers, only 8 (1.6 per cent) were aware of the Minimum Wages Act while the remaining majority (99.4 per cent) were ignorant of it. The reason for this sorry state of affairs is the to lack of education and prevalance of illiteracy among women labourers.

Comparatively speaking, the awareness level is nearly equal among the women labourers of both developed and underdeveloped villages (1.3 per cent from the developed villages and 2.1 per cent from the underdeveloped villages).

With regard to the system of wage distribution, it was stated by the majority of the women labourers (89.2 per cent) that they received their wages directly from their employers whereas another 7.8 per cent did so from the contractors. The agents also reported to be distributing the wages in the case of 3 per cent women labourers.

Table 5.31. Awareness about the Minimum Wage Act and the System of Wage Distribution

Block	Village	Awareness			System of Wage Distribution		
		Yes	No	Total	Employer	Agent	Contractor
	Developed						
Athoor	1. Athoor	1 (0.7)	151 (99.3)	152	145 (95.4)	6 (4.0)	1 (0.6)
R.Chatram	2. S.Vadipatti	1 (1.1)	89 (98.9)	90	90 (100.0)	---	---
Dindigul	3. Chatrapatti	2 (3.0)	65 (97.0)	67	37 (55.2)	9 (13.4)	21 (31.4)
Total (A)		4 (1.3)	305 (98.7)	309 (61.8)	272 (88.0)	15 (4.8)	22 (7.1)
	Underdeveloped						
Athoor	1. Indirapuram	1 (1.5)	64 (98.5)	65	65 (100.0)	---	---
R.Chatram	2. Kathiriyankulam	---	63 (100.0)	63	61 (96.8)	---	2 (3.2)
Dindigul	3 Kiriyampatti	3 (4.8)	60 (95.2)	63	48 (76.2)	---	15 (23.8)
	Total (B)	4 (2.1)	187 (97.9)	191 (38.2)	174 (91.1)	---	17 (8.9)
	Grand Total (A+B)	8 (1.6)	492 (98.4)	500 (100.0)	446 (89.2)	15 (3.0)	39 (7.8)

Source: Computed from primary data

* Figures in parantheses indicate percentages (Multiple responses)

Figure VII

Awareness about the Minimum Wage Act

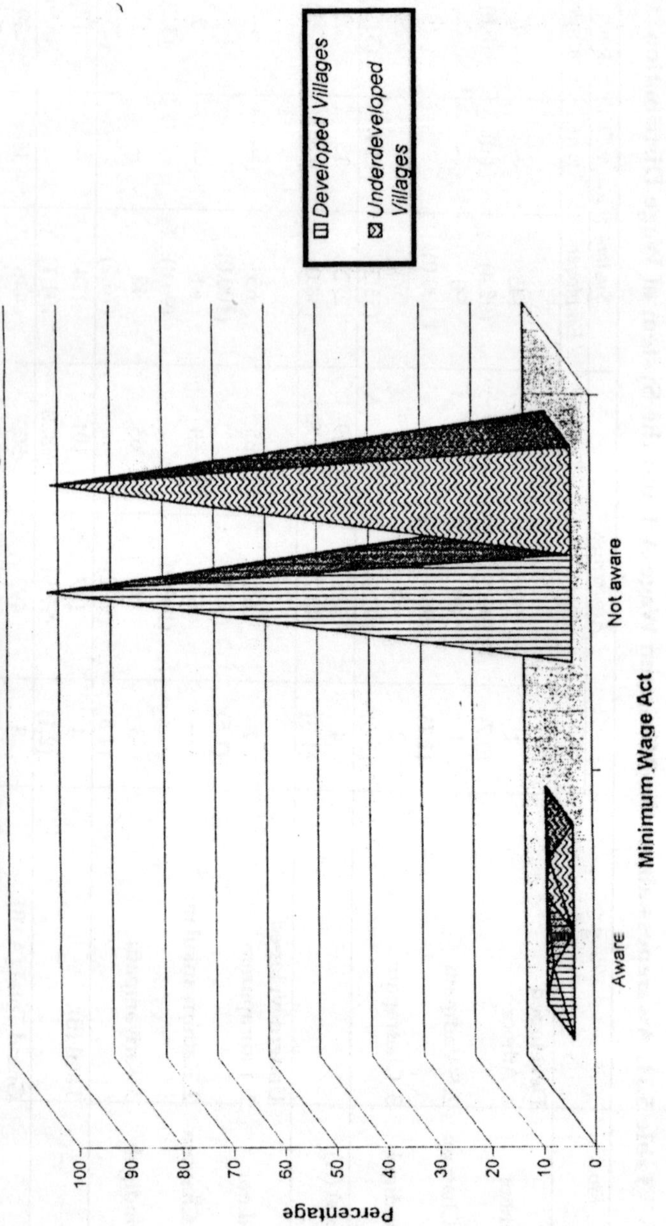

Group-wise there is only a slight difference: while 91.1 per cent of the women labourers from the underdeveloped villages receive their wages from the employers, the percentage is 88 per cent in the developed villages; 8.9 per cent of the women labourers from the underdeveloped villages and 7.1 per cent from the developed villages get their wages from the contractors; but, all the 15 women labourers who get their wages from the agents are only from the developed villages.

It is really a sorry state of affairs that only eight women labourers (out of the 500) were aware of the Minimum Wages Act. This necessitates a wider publicity and education of the workers about the various provisions and facilities due to the workers including the provisions of the Minimum Wages Act.

The majority of the respondents (89 per cent) receive their wages directly from their employer since the majority of them work as labourers in the agricultural sector.

(iii) Problems Related to in Home Management

Husbands Role and Home Management by Women Labourers

Marital status is an important determinant of women's employment. In rural areas, women labourers are allowed to work only on the willingness and acceptance of their husband. Table 5.32 the opinion of husbands regarding the women labourers' work. All the 415 married women labourers were asked about the opinion of their husbands regarding their work. To this, 97.1 per cent replied that their husbands accepted and allowed the working of their wives (respondents) whereas the remaining 2.9 per cent said that their husbands do not accept and allow their wives to work.

The respondents whose husbands accept their working were asked for the reasons. Additional income was a major factor that made 72.5 per cent of their husbands allow their wives to work. Sharing the family expenditure was the reason for 50.1 per cent of the husbands to permit their wives to go for work. Saving for future and creating assets for future generation (21.3 per cent), main source of family income (5.5 per cent) and employment within the village (6.2 per cent) were the other reasons that motivated their husbands to agree to the work of their wives. With regard to the non-acceptance of the wives' work, the prevailing very low wage rates both inside and outside villages (75.0 per cent) and the need for hard work (25 per cent) were stated as the reasons.

Group-wise, almost equal percentage of husbands from both the category of villages allowed their wives to work both inside and outside the villages. With regard to the reasons, a higher percentage of women labourers from the developed villages have reported sharing family expenditure (56.0 per cent), asset creation (25.4 per cent), main source of family income (8.1 per cent), and, employment within the village (6.8 per cent) as the major reasons. The women labourers from underdeveloped villages have stated additional income (83.9 per cent) as a reason. Allowing the wife to work and earn will increase the family income and, more particularly, ensure the economic independence of women folk. The major reasons for their acceptance includes additional income for the family (72.5 per cent), and sharing family expenditure (50.1 per cent). This attitude of the husbands to permit their wives to work and earn is a good sign of development. The reasons for not permitting their wives to work by a few husbands are not very serious, i.e., low rate of wage and need for hard work. If these hurdles are overcome, probably they will also permit their wives to work. Thus women labourers in the study area directly help in enhancing the economic status of the family and indirectly help in promoting the levels of living.

If the husbands are satisfied with the working hours of the wives there will be no problems and, if they are not satisfied, there is a chance of friction or petty quarrels within the family. Table 5.33 shows the husbands' satisfaction towards working timings of the women labourers. Of the 415 respondents living

Table 5.32. Husbands' Acceptance of Wives' Work

Block	Village	Acceptance			Reasons for Acceptance					Reasons for non-acceptance *	
		Yes	No	Total	1	2	3	4	5	a	b
	Developed										
Athoor	1. Athoor	122 (97.6)	3 (2.4)	125	52 (42.6)	76 (62.3)	42 (34.4)	17 (14.0)	10 (8.2)	2 (66.7)	1 (33.3)
R.Chatram	2. S.Vadipatti	71 (98.6)	1 (1.4)	72	65 (91.5)	40 (56.3)	13 (18.3)	---	---	1	---
Dindigul	3. Chatrapatti	55 (93.2)	4 (6.8)	59	45 (81.8)	23 (41.8)	8 (14.5)	3 (5.4)	7 (12.7)	3 (75.0)	1 (25.0)
Total (A)		248 (96.9)	8 (3.1)	256 (61.7)	162 (65.3)	139 (56.0)	63 (25.4)	20 (8.1)	17 (6.8)	6 (75.0)	2 (25.0)
	Underdeveloped										
Athoor	1. Indirapuram	49 (96.0)	2 (4.0)	51	44 (89.8)	20 (40.8)	8 (16.3)	---	---	1	1
R.Chatram	2. Kathiriyankulam	55 (100.0)	---	55	40 (72.7)	21 (38.2)	9 (16.4)	---	6 (10.9)	---	---
Dindigul	3. Kiriyampatti	51 (96.2)	2 (3.8)	53	46 (90.2)	22 (43.1)	6 (11.8)	2 (3.9)	2 (3.9)	2	---
	Total (B)	155 (97.5)	4 (2.5)	159 (38.3)	130 (83.9)	63 (40.6)	23 (14.8)	2 (1.3)	8 (5.2)	3 (75.0)	1 (25.0)
	Grand Total (A+B)	403 (97.1)	12 (2.9)	415 (100.0)	292 (72.5)	202 (50.1)	86 (21.3)	22 (5.5)	25 (6.2)	9 (75.0)	3 (25.0)

Source: Computed from primary data * Figures in parantheses indicate percentages (Multiple responses)

1. Additional Income; 2. Sharing family expenditure; 3. Saving and creating asset; 4. Main source of family income; 5. Employment within the village. a. Very low wage b. Hard work

with their husbands, nine-tenths (90.1 per cent) felt happy that their husbands were satisfied with their working hours whereas the remaining 9.9 per cent were not satisfied.

With regard to the reasons for satisfaction, four-fifths (80 per cent) stated that the timing of working hours was fixed and this helps to plan the activities of husband and wife. This fixed timing enables them to carry out their routine activities without any disturbance. Another 48.7 per cent felt that the working time was suitable for women labourers whereas 19 per cent of them were happy that the women work only during the day time.

Similarly, those women labourers whose husbands were not satisfied with the working hours were requested to spell out the major reasons. Both the husbands and wives having to work during the same hours was the main reason expressed by 49.0 per cent of them. Because of identical hours of working, both the husbands and wives have to be away from home and could not spare time and service for household and other domestic activities. Longer hours of work was the reason for the dissatisfaction of 49 per cent of the husbands. Child care was possible was the reason given by 43.9 per cent of the husbands for their dissatisfaction.

The economic condition of rural workers is poor and the earning of either the husband or the wife is not sufficient to meet even the basic needs of the family. The trend is that the females also have to work to supplement the family income. Though the husbands expect their wives to earn, there are instances where the husbands are not satisfied about the amount earned by their wives.

Table 5.34 reveals the husband's satisfaction about the present wage rate of their wives. In this study, of the 415 respondents living with their husbands nine-tenths (91.6 per cent) have expressed that their husbands are satisfied with their wages. The remaining (8.4 per cent) of the respondents' husbands are not satisfied. As for the reason for their satisfaction, three-

Table 5.33. Husband's Attitude towards Working Timings of Women Labourers

Block	*Village*	*Satisfied*	*Dis-satisfied*	*Total*	*Reasons for satisfaction*			*Reason for dissatisfaction*		
					1	*2*	*3*	*a*	*b*	*c*
	Developed									
Athoor	1. Athoor	122 (97.6)	3 (2.4)	125	99 (81.1)	68 (55.7)	13 (10.6)	1 (33.3)	2 (66.7)	---
R.Chatram	2. S.Vadipatti	71 (98 6)	1 (1.4)	72	49 (69.1)	37 (52.0)	17 (23.9)	1 (100.0)	---	---
Dindigul	3. Chatrapatti	55 (93.2)	4 (6.8)	59	41 (74.5)	24 (43.6)	8 (14.5)	2 (50.0)	1 (25.0)	1 (25.0)
	Total (A)	248 (96.9)	8 (3.1)	256 (61.7)	189 (76.2)	129 (52.0)	38 (15.3)	4 (50.0)	3 (37.5)	1 (12.5)
	Underdeveloped									
Athoor	1. Indirapuram	33 (64.7)	18 (35.3)	51	31 (93.9)	18 (54.5)	10 (30.3)	5 (27.8)	10 (55.5)	3 (16.7)
R.Chatram	2. Kathiriyankulam	54 (98.2)	1 (1.8)	55	50 (92.6)	13 (24.1)	5 (9.2)	1 (100.0)	---	---
Dindigul	3. Kiriyampatti	39 (73.6)	14 (26.4)	53	29 (74.3)	22 (56.4)	18 (46.1)	10 (71.4)	7 (50.0)	14 (100.0)
	Total (B)	126 (79.2)	33 (20.7)	159 (38.3)	110 (87.3)	53 (42.1)	33 (26.2)	16 (48.5)	17 (51.5)	17 (51.5)
	Grand Total (A+B)	374 (90.1)	41 (9.9)	415 (100.0)	299 (80.0)	182 (48.7)	71 (19.0)	20 (49.0)	20 (49.0)	18 (43.9)

Source: Computed from primary data   * Figures in parantheses indicate percentages (Multiple responses)

1. Fixed timing in the area; 2. Suitability for women; 3. Work during day time (a) Same hours of working (b) Longer hours of work (c) Child care not possible.

Table 5.34. Husbands' Satisfaction about Present Wage of the Wife

Block	Village	Response		Reasons for satisfaction				Reasons for dissatisfaction		
		Satisfied	Dissatis fied	Fixed wage	Additiona l Income	To run the family	No other way	Un emplo- yed	Low income	In sufficient wage
	Developed									
Athoor	1. Athoor	118 (94.4)	7 (5.6)	70 (59.3)	66 (55.9)	33 (28.0)	22 (18.6)	1 (0.8)	2 (28.6)	5 (71.4)
R.Chatram	2. S.Vadipatti	69 (95.8)	3 (4.2)	58 (40.6)	42 (60.9)	22 (31.9)	----	---	2 (66.6)	3 (100.0)
Dindigul	3. Chatrapatti	47 (79.7)	12 (20.3)	33 (70.2)	19 (40.4)	14 (29.8)	4 (8.5)	---	5 (41.7)	7 (58.3)
	Total (A)	234 (91.4)	22 (8.6)	161 (68.8)	127 (54.3)	69 (29.5)	26 (11.1)	1 (4.5)	9 (40.9)	15 (68.2)
	Underdeveloped									
Athoor	1. Indirapuram	44 (86.3)	7 (13.7)	29 (65.9)	20 (45.4)	12 (27.3)	---	---	4 (57.1)	3 (42.8)
R.Chatram	2. Kathiriyankulam	54 (98.2)	1 (1.8)	47 (87.0)	13 (24.0)	8 (14.8)	--	2 (3.7)	---	1 (100.0)
Dindigul	3. Kiriyampatti	48 (90.6)	5 (9.4)	41 (85.4)	25 (52.1)	5 (10.4)	1 (2.0)	1 (2.0)	5 (100.0)	1 (20.0)
	Total (B)	146 (91.8)	13 (8.2)	117 (80.1)	58 (39.7)	25 (17.1)	1 (0.7)	3 (23.1)	9 (69.2)	5 (38.5)
	Grand Total (A+B)	380 (91.6)	35 (8.4)	278 (73.1)	185 (48.7)	94 (24.7)	27 (7.1)	4 (1.0)	18 (51.4)	20 (57.1)

Source: Computed from primary data

* Figures in parantheses indicate percentages (Multiple responses)

fourths (73.1 per cent) felt that whether they get higher or lower income they get a fixed wage for their work and get regular income and hence the families are able to get an additional income in the case of 48.7 per cent women labourers; this income helps the women labourers to run the family (24.7 per cent); another 7.1 per cent are satisfied because there is no other way except getting this income; and, in the case of four (1.0 per cent) respondents, their husbands are unemployed and so they have to be satisfied with whatever their wives earn.

With regard to the reason for dissatisfaction, 57.1 per cent felt that the wage rate is insufficient and they do not get the wage proportionate to their work. The family income of another 51.4 per cent is already low and so their husbands are not satisfied with the wage rate of their wives. Insufficient wage rate for the heavy work (68.2 per cent from the developed villages) and low income (69.2 per cent from the underdeveloped villages) are the reasons spelt out by the women labourers for the dissatisfaction of their husbands about the wage rate of their wives.

Group-wise, in both the types of villages, the percentage of women labourers reporting their husband's satisfaction over the present wage rate is almost equal. The husbands of 80.1 per cent from the underdeveloped villages are satisfied because their wives are able to get fixed wage rate in the study area while 68.8 per cent from the developed villages are so and 54.3 per cent from developed villages say their families get additional income while 39.7 per cent from underdeveloped villages say so. The majority of the husbands of the women labourers (91.8 per cent) were satisfied about the wage their wives get now. Fixed wage as income (73.1 per cent), additional income (48.7 per cent), help in running family (24.7 per cent) are the major reasons for their satisfaction.

Disproportionate wage, poor family income are the reasons for their husbands' dissatisfaction about their wives' wage rate. The Govt. machinery must be motivated to see that the Minimum

Table 5.35. Contribution of Husbands' Earnings to the Family of Women Labourers

Block	*Village*	*Contribute to Family*		*Reasons for not paid*		
		Yes	*No*	*Drinking habit*	*Smoking habit*	*Personal Expenses*
	Developed					
Athoor	1. Athoor	108 (86.4)	17 (13.6)	13 (76.5)	12 (70-6)	10 (58.8)
R.Chatram	2. S.Vadipatti	65 (90.3)	7 (9.7)	7 (100.0)	4 (57.1)	3 (42.8)
Dindigul	3. Chatrapatti	40 (67.8)	19 (32.2)	11 (57.9)	6 (31.6)	5 (26.3)
	Total (A)	213 (83.2)	43 (16.8)	31 (72.1)	22 (51.2)	18 (41.9)
	Underdeveloped					
Athoor	1. Indirapuram	29 (56.9)	22 (43.1)	15 (68.2)	10 (45.4)	7 (31.8)
R.Chatram	2. Kathiriyankulam	45 (81.8)	10 (18.2)	1 (10.0)	4 (40.0)	5 (50.0)
Dindigul	3. Kiriyampatti	42 (79.2)	11 (20.8)	5 (45.4)	4 (36.4)	4 (36.4)
	Total (B)	116 (73.0)	43 (27.0)	21 (48.8)	18 (41.9)	16 (37.2)
	Grand Total (A+B)	329 (79.3)	86 (20.7)	52 (60.5)	40 (46.5)	34 (39.5)

Source: Computed from primary data

* Figures in parantheses indicate percentages (Multiple responses)

Wages Act is implemented well and to safeguard the interests of the women labourers.

Generally, the earning males tend to spend a portion of their earnings for their personal activities like having coffee, tea, betel leaf and nut, smoking, drinking and entertaining friends or colleagues etc. Table 5.35 deals with the contribution of husbands' earnings to the family of the women labourers. The respondents were enquired whether their husbands contributed their entire earnings to the family. It is interesting to note that, among the 415 women labourers living with their husbands, 79.3 per cent revealed that their husbands handed over their entire earnings to the family. The remaining (20.7 per cent) gave a negative response that they are not able to get the entire amount earned by their husbands. These women labourers attributed some reasons for this. Their husbands spent money for drinking alcohol, as stated by 60.5 per cent; smoking consumes some amount of earning, as expressed by 46.5 per cent of the women labourers; some males used the money on some personal expenses like having coffee, tea and buying lottery tickets and this was stated by 39.5 per cent women labourers.

Group-wise, 27.0 per cent of the women labourers from underdeveloped villages reported that their husbands do not contribute their entire earnings to the family, whereas it is only 16.8 per cent of the women labourers from the developed villages who complained about their husbands' non-contribution. With regard to reasons, a higher percentage of respondents from the developed villages have attributed that their husbands have developed drinking habit (72.1 per cent), smoking habit (51.2 per cent), and incurred personal expenses (41.9 per cent) while the percentages are lower among the respondents from underdeveloped villages (48.8 per cent, 41.9 per cent and 37.2 per cent respectively).

To avoid unnecessary expenditure by their husbands and to meet the increasing financial needs of the family, the women need to get the entire earnings of their husbands. In this respect,

Figure VIII
Contribution of Husbands' Earning

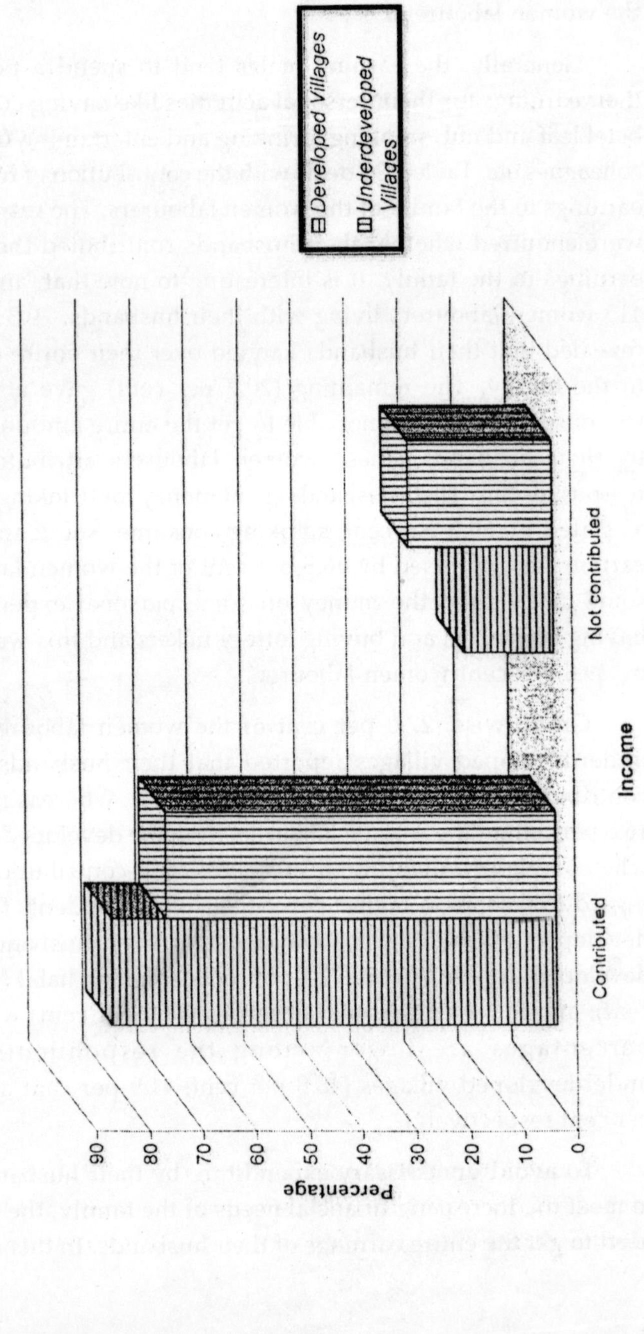

the women labourers (79.3 per cent) living with their husbands were able to get the entire earnings of their husbands (83 per cent from developed villages and 73 per cent from underdeveloped villages).

Spending on alcohol and smoking are the major types of unnecessary and unhealthy expenses which divert a portion of male earnings. So, steps must be taken to create awareness about the evil effect of alcoholism and smoking.

It has become a customary practice among the males to cultivate some types of unhealthy habits like drinking alcohol, smoking, chewing betelnut etc. These habits not only lead to health hazards but also involve personal expenditure. Table 5.36 shows the personal habits and expenditure incurred by the husbands of the women labourers. The women labourers of this study were enquired whether their husbands have any such habits. It is seen that 33.8 per cent of the women labourers have a positive reply stating that their husbands have one or two such habits. Among these husbands, 69.2 per cent were reported to have the habit of smoking while more than half of the husbands (55.0 per cent) were addicted to alcohol. (Problems experienced by the wives of alcoholics, 90.8 per cent women reported they had to take earner responsibilities to over come the financial constraints arising out of the husbands drinking. Nearly half of them reported that they started to work only because of the husband's addiction to alcohol consumption, clearance of debts accumulated by the husband became solely their responsibility (N.Kamalamma and K.S. Pushpa 1997). Betelnut chewing was also one of the habits cultivated by 18.9 per cent of the husbands.

Group-wise, nearly three-fifths of the women labourers (58.6 per cent) from the developed villages reported their husbands having some of these habits. More number of husbands from the developed villages were reported to have drinking habits (55.5 per cent) and betelnut chewing (26.3 per cent) whereas the number of husbands with smoking habit was more (63.6 per cent) in the underdeveloped villages.

With regard to the expenditure incurred on these habits, it is a sorry state of affairs: a little less than one-third of the husbands (30.8 per cent) spent more than Rs. 200 per month; another 28.4 per cent spent an amount between Rs. 51 to Rs.100 per month; the amount spent by 25.4 per cent of the husbands on these unhealthy habits was in the range of Rs.101 to Rs.150 per month; and, it was Rs.151-Rs.200 in the case of 8.9 per cent of the husbands. Only a meagre 6.5 per cent reported to have spent an amount of Rs. 50 and below per month.

Group-wise, the highest amount of Rs.200 and above is being spent by more number of husbands (38.6 per cent) from the underdeveloped villages and another 28.5 per cent from the underdeveloped villages have reported to spend Rs.101-Rs.150 per month. The lowest amount of Rs. 50 and less has been reported by more number of husbands (8.1 per cent) from the developed villages.

The womenfolk of Indian villages have many advantages in working with their husbands. The women labourers were asked whether they used to work together with their husbands and their responses are presented in Table 5.37. Of the respondents living with their husbands, only one-tenth (11.3 per cent) have responded that they work with their husbands while the remaining majority (88.7 per cent) do not join their husbands but work separately.

With regard to the advantages of working together, the majority of those working with their husbands (57.4 per cent) have experienced sharing of work between husbands and wife as an advantage. Security to the woman worker, was another advantage stated by 53.2 per cent. It enables sharing of lunch as stated by 15 per cent of the women labourers.

A little less than three-fourths of the respondents (10.5 per cent) from the developed villages and only a little above two-fifths (12.6 per cent) from the underdeveloped villages have stated that they work along with their husbands.

Table 5.36. Personal Habits and Unwanted Expenditure Incurred by Husbands

Block	Village	1	2	Personal habits *			Expenditure (Monthly in Rs)				
				3	4	5	6	7	8	9	10
	Developed										
Athoor	1. Athoor	152	69 (45.4)	32 (46.4)	51 (73.9)	8 (11.6)	8 (11.6)	30 (43.5)	8 (11.6)	7 (10.1)	16 (23.2)
.Chatram	2. S.Vadipatti	90	10 (11.1)	9 (90.0)	4 (40.0)	6 (60.0)	---	---	7 (70.0)	---	3 (30.0)
Dindigul	3. Chatrapatti	67	20 (29.8)	14 (70.0)	8 (40.0)	12 (60.0)	---	---	8 (40.0)	6 (30.0)	6 (30.0)
	Total (A)	309 (61.8)	99 (32.0)	55 (55.5)	63 (63.6)	26 (26.3)	8 (8.1)	30 (30.3)	23 (23.2)	13 (13.1)	25 (25.2)
	Underdeveloped										
Athoor	1. Indirapuram	65	26 (40.0)	26 (100.0)	14 (53.8)	1 (3.8)	---	1 (3.8)	4 (15.4)	2 (7.7)	19 (73.1)
R.Chatram	2. Kathiriyankulam	63	22 (34.9)	5 (22.7)	22 (100.0)	---	---	10 (45.4)	8 (36.3)	---	4 (18.2)
Dindigul	3. Kiriyampatti	63	22 (35.0)	7 (31.8)	18 (81.8)	5 (22.7)	3 (13.6)	7 (31.8)	8 (36.4)	---	4 (18.2)
	Total (B)	191 (38.2)	70 (36.6)	38 (54.3)	54 (77.1)	6 (8.5)	3 (4.3)	18 (25.7)	20 (28.6)	2 (2.9)	27 (38.6)
	Grand Total (A+B)	500 (100.0)	169 (33.8)	93 (55.0)	117 (69.2)	32 (18.9)	11 (6.5)	48 (28.4)	43 (25.4)	15 (8.9)	52 (30.8)

Source: Computed from primary data * Figures in parantheses indicate percentages (Multiple responses)

1. No. of Respondents, 2. No. of Respondents having habits, 3. Drinking, 4. Smoking, 5. Bettelnut, 6. Upto Rs. 50, 7. Rs. 51-100, 8. Rs. 101-150, 9. Rs. 151-200, 10. Above Rs. 200.

It is inferred from the above analysis that though some of the women labourers are aware of the advantages of working with their husbands, they could not get employment chances for both of them in the same place. But, at the same time, these women labourers are courageous to go alone with other workers to work.

Generally, in rural areas, the patriarchal family system prevails and the prevalence of gender discrimination exists due to ignorance, low social status and illiteracy among women. Males, especially those who are in the low strata, are in the habit of incurring unnecessary and unwanted expenditure and this aggravates their economic problems further. Table 5.38 reveals the problems faced by women labourers with their husbands.

When the women labourers were asked to spell out whether they faced any problems with their husbands, 27.6 per cent reported to have some problems with their husbands. Consumption of alcohol (58.7 per cent) and smoking (50.0 per cent) were the major problems with their husbands and the other problems included petty quarrels (19.6 per cent) and scolding unnecessarily (21.0 per cent). They also suggested some methods to solve their problems: 68.8 per cent suggested avoiding the drinking habit (alcohol) by their husbands; careful and planned spending of money was suggested by 47.1 per cent; one-third (33.3 per cent) stated that the husbands should cooperate with their wives in day-to-day activities.

Group-wise, a little less than one-third (31.9 per cent) from the underdeveloped villages and one fourth (4.9 per cent) from the developed villages reported a few problems with their husbands. Among the women labourers from the developed villages, the major problem was smoking (74.0 per cent) followed by drinking alcohol (61.0 per cent), petty quarrel (31.2 per cent) and scolding (18.2 per cent). In the case of the underdeveloped villages, the major problem was alcoholism (55.7 per cent) followed by scolding (24.6 per cent), smoking (19.7 per cent) and quarreling (4.9 per cent).

Table 5.37. Respondent Working Together with Husband and Its Advantages

Block	Village	Work Together		Advantages in working Together *		
		Yes	No	Sharing of work	Security	Sharing of lunch
	Developed					
Athoor	1. Athoor	17 (13.6)	108 (86.4)	4 (23.5)	6 (35.3)	3 (17.6)
R.Chatram	2. S.Vadipatti	2 (2.8)	70 (97.2)	1 (50.0)	1 (50.0)	---
Dindigul	3. Chatrapatti	8 (13.6)	51 (86.4)	4 (50.0)	6 (75.0)	3 (37.5)
	Total (A)	27 (10.5)	229 (89.5)	9 (33.3)	13 (48.1)	6 (22.2)
	Underdeveloped					
Athoor	1. Indirapuram	4 (7.8)	47 (92.2)	4 (100.0)	---	---
R.Chatram	2. Kathiriyankulam	3 (5.5)	52 (94.5)	2 (50.0)	2 (50.0)	---
Dindigul	3. Kiriyampatti	13 (24.5)	40 (75.5)	12 (92.3)	10 (76.9)	1 (7.7)
	Total (B)	20 (12.6)	139 (87.4)	18 (90.0)	12 (60.0)	1 (5.0)
	Grand Total (A+B)	47 (11.3)	368 (88.7)	27 (57.4)	25 (53.2)	7 (15.0)

Source: Computed from primary data

* Figures in parantheses indicate percentages (Multiple responses)

Table 5.38. Nature of Problems with Husbands and Methods of Settlement

Block	Village	Total Respondents	Respondents having problems	Type of Problems				Settlement of Problem		
				1	2	3	4	a	b	c
	Developed									
Athoor	1. Athoor	152	44 (35.2)	34 (77.3)	33 (75.0)	---	---	23 (52.3)	---	18 (40.9)
R.Chatram	2.S.Vadipatti	90	16 (22.2)	13 (81.3)	12 (75.0)	13 (81.3)	---	14 (87.5)	12 (75.0)	10 (62.5)
Dindigul	3.Chatrapatti	67	17 (31.0)	---	12 (70.6)	11 (64.7)	14 (82.4)	12 (70.6)	11 (64.7)	14 (82.4)
Total (A)		309 (61.8)	77 (24.9)	47 (61.0)	57 (74.0)	24 (31.2)	14 (18.2)	49 (63.6)	23 (29.9)	42 (54.5)
	Underdeveloped									
Athoor	1.Indirapuram	65	25 (49.0)	13 (52.0)	12 (48.0)	---	---	24 (96.0)	11 (44.0)	8 (32.0)
R.Chatram	2.Kathiriyankulam	63	23 (42.0)	12 (52.2)	---	---	11 (47.8)	14 (60.9)	12 (52.2)	10 (43.5)
Dindigul	3.Kiriyampatti	63	13 (24.5)	9 (69.3)	---	3 (23.1)	4 (30.8)	8 (61.5)	---	5 (38.5)
	Total (B)	191 (38.2)	61 (31.9)	34 (55.7)	12 (19.7)	3 (4.9)	15 (24.6)	46 (75.4)	23 (37.7)	23 (37.7)
	Grand Total (A+B)	500 (100.0)	138 (27.6)	81 (58.7)	69 (50.0)	27 (19.6)	29 (21.0)	95 (68.8)	46 (33.3)	65 (47.1)

Source: Computed from primary data * Figures in parantheses indicate percentages (Multiple responses)

1. Drinking, 2. Smoking, 3. Quarrel, 4. Scolding, a. Avoid Drinking, b. Cooperate with wife, c. Careful in spending money.

Figure IX
Nature of Problems with Husbands

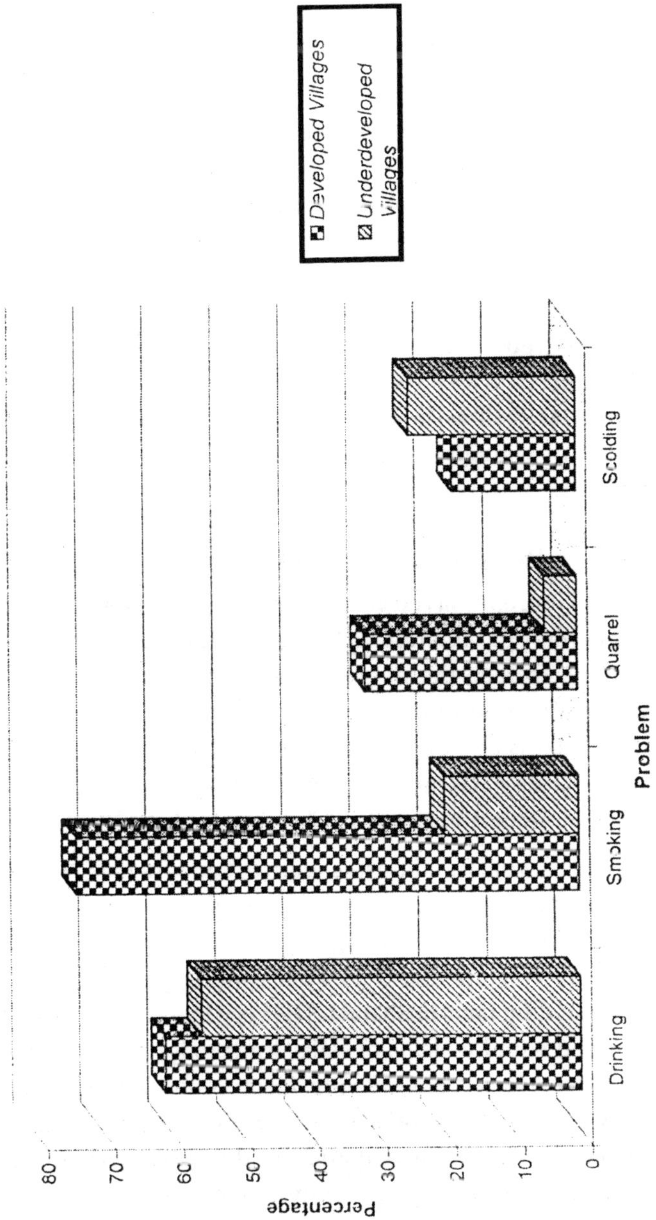

Group-wise, 24.9 per cent from the developed villages and 31.9 per cent from the underdeveloped villages reported to have some problems. Alcoholism was the major problem in underdeveloped villages, while smoking was reported as the major problem in the developed villages.

These types of major problems, that is spending money on alcoholism and smoking, resulted in waste of money and it also affected the health. In order to save money and health, NGOs must come forward with good proposals to introduce some kind of social and moral education to the family members in general and husbands in particular in the study area. Schemes like Micro Credit (MC) and Self Help Groups (SHG) could be introduced in the study region so as to cultivate the habit of saving as well as to start micro business enterprises. This may result in changing the social habits of the individuals in the villages.

Role of Women Labourers in Family Decision

The role played by women in the family and community are certain parameters which reflect the status of women in the society. In fact, the degree of involvement in decision making process related to family matters can serve as a good indicator of the status of women in households, which, in turn, determines their status in the society. Table 5.39 depicts the involvement of women labourers in family decision making by their husbands.

The women labourers were asked whether their husbands consult their wives on important family matters. To this, 75.6 per cent of the total respondents answered positively, stating that they are consulted and 24.4 per cent reported that they are not consulted by their husbands. The very low level of female literacy, coupled with low level of skills, leads to low level of employment and low wages. Consequently, their economic status gets lowered, affecting their general status, and thus, they get pushed behind in the process of participation in decision making, which is an unavoidable feature of family management, which ultimately

Table 5.39. Involvement of Women Labourers in Family Decision Making

Block	*Village*	*Involvement*			*Reasons for not consultation **		
		Yes	*No*	*No.of Respondents*	*No Idea*	*Customary practice*	*Being female*
	Developed						
Athoor	1. Athoor	121 (79.6)	31 (20.4)	152	23 (74.2)	12 (38.7)	13 (41.9)
R.Chatram	2.S.Vadipatti	53 (58.9)	37 (41.1)	90	16 (43.2)	17 (45.9)	9 (24.3)
Dindigul	3.Chatrapatti	54 (80.6)	13 (19.4)	67	8 (61.5)	2 (15.4)	7 (53.8)
Total (A)		228 (73.8)	81 (26.2)	309 (61.8)	47 (58.0)	31 (38.3)	29 (35.8)
	Underdeveloped						
Athoor	1.Indirapuram	46 (70.8)	19 (29.8)	65	9 (47.4)	10 (52.6)	5 (26.3)
R.Chatram	2.Kathiriyankulam	54 (85.7)	9 (14.3)	63	5 (55.5)	4 (44.4)	2 (22.2)
Dindigul	3.Kiriyampatti	50 (79.4)	13 (20.6)	63	7 (53.8)	4 (30.8)	2 (15.3)
	Total (B)	150 (78.5)	41 (21.5)	191 (38.2)	21 (51.2)	18 (43.9)	9 (21.9)
	Grand Total (A+B)	378 (75.6)	122 (24.4)	500 (100.0)	68 (55.7)	49 (40.2)	38 (31.1)

Source: Computed from primary data

* Figures in parantheses indicate percentages (Multiple responses)

determines its quality. (Mohanty and Samantaray 1997). With regard to the reasons, more than half of the respondents (55.7 per cent) were ignorant and they stated that they do not know the actual reason, whereas 40.2 per cent explained that it is a customary practice not to consult the womenfolk on important family matters. Another 31.1 per cent of these women labourers regretted that their husbands do not consult them just because they are females.

Group-wise, 78.5 per cent of the women labourers from the underdeveloped villages and 73.8 per cent of the women labourers from developed villages reported that they are being consulted on important family matters. More than half of the respondents (51.2 per cent) from the underdeveloped villages showed ignorance about the reasons for their not being consulted, whereas the same type of response came from 58.0 per cent of the women labourers from developed villages. That this is customary practice was reported by 43.9 per cent of the women labourers from underdeveloped villages and 38.3 per cent from developed villages. The reason that they are not consulted just because they are females was stated by 35.8 per cent from the developed and 21.9 per cent from the underdeveloped villages.

In the decision making process on important family matters, 75.6 per cent of the women labourers expressed their emotional satisfaction that they are given due recognition in such important matters.

The inference is that their recognition and involvement is mainly due to their share in the economic aspects of the family. The women, per se, need to be given due respect and should be consulted on all matters. It is pathetic to note that there are a considerable number of women without knowing the reason for their not being consulted. This situation should be changed by providing proper awareness about their role, rights and responsibilities in the family. At the same time, the males should also be sensitised against gender discrimination and urged to give equal status to women in the family.

Care and Support by Husband

In rural areas, the women labourers are socially and economically very low in power. When women fall sick, the husbands are supposed to take care of them and also assist their wives in household and other activities. Table 5.40 indicates the nature of care of women labourers by husbands during illness.

Among the 500 women labourers, 415 (83.0 per cent) were with their husbands and the remaining were either unmarried, widowed, separated or destitute. These 415 respondents were asked whether their husbands render any assistance and help during their illness. To this, three-fourths (74.0 per cent) provided affirmative responses, whereas the remaining 26 per cent reported non-assistance. The women labourers were further enquired about the type of help and assistance received from their husbands. Taking the wife to the hospital was the major type of assistance, stated by 92.5 per cent of the women labourers; providing medicine during illness was been stated to be an other type of help received by 61.9 per cent of the women labourers; the other types of help included sharing family and household work (20.8 per cent) and just taking care of the wife (14.6 per cent). A comparative analysis shows that taking wife to hospital has been stated by almost an equal percentage of women labourers (93.4 per cent in the developed villages and 91.0 per cent in the underdeveloped villages). Providing medicine as a help was expressed by more respondents (65.3 per cent) in the developed villages than from underdeveloped villages (55.9 per cent).

On the contrary, sharing the family work is done by more husbands (26.1 per cent) in the underdeveloped villages than in the developed villages (17.9 per cent).

With regard to the reasons for non-assistance by the husbands, 76.8 per cent stated that their husbands generally neglect them during illness which may be because of their quarrels, heavy work etc. Another 40.7 per cent reported that their husbands used to ill treat them in an alcoholic mood because they don't like their wives to fall ill.

Table 5.40. Care of Women Labourers by Husbands during Illness

Block	Village	Assistance			Nature of help				Reasons for not Assisting	
		Given	Not given	Total	1	2	3	4	a	b
	Developed									
Athoor	1. Athoor	101 (80.7)	24 (19.3)	125	94 (93.1)	70 (69.3)	8 (7.9)	18 (17.8)	16 (66.7)	9 (37.5)
R.Chatram	2.S.Vadipatti	46 (63.9)	26 (36.1)	72	44 (95.6)	39 (84.7)	7 (15.2)	9 (19.6)	17 (65.3)	12 (46.1)
Dindigul	3.Chatrapatti	49 (83.1)	10 (16.9)	59	45 (91.8)	19 (38.8)	5 (10.2)	8 (16.3)	8 (80.0)	2 (20.0)
	Total (A)	196 (76.6)	60 (23.4)	256 (61.7)	183 (93.4)	128 (65.3)	20 (10.2)	35 (17.9)	41 (68.3)	23 (38.3)
	Underdeveloped									
Athoor	1.Indirapuram	32 (62.7)	19 (37.3)	51	30 (93.7)	27 (84.3)	7 (21.9)	15 (46.8)	17 (89.5)	2 (10.5)
R.Chatram	2.Kathiriyankulam	43 (78.2)	12 (21.8)	55	35 (81.4)	6 (13.9)	12 (27.9)	10 (23.2)	10 (83.3)	7 (58.3)
Dindigul	3.Kiriyampatti	36 (67.9)	17 (32.1)	53	36 (100.0)	29 (80.5)	6 (16.7)	4 (11.1)	15 (88.2)	12 (70.6)
	Total (B)	111 (69.8)	48 (30.2)	159 (38.3)	101 (91.0)	62 (55.9)	25 (22.5)	29 (26.1)	42 (87.5)	21 (43.7)
	Grand Total (A+B)	307 (74.0)	108 (26.0)	415 (100.0)	284 (92.5)	190 (61.9)	45 (14.6)	64 (20.8)	83 (76.8)	44 (40.7)

Source: Computed from primary data * Figures in parantheses indicate percentages (Multiple responses)

1. Takes to Hospital, 2. Provides medicine, 3. Care, 4. Sharing family work, a. Neglect during illness, b. Illtreatment.

Table 5.41. Care of Women Labourers by Husbands during Illness

Block	*Village*	*Support*		*Nature of Support*				
		Yes	*No*	*1*	*2*	*3*	*4*	*5*
	Developed							
Athoor	1. Athoor	120 (96.0)	5 (4.0)	27 (22.5)	44 (36.7)	104 (86.7)	17 (14.2)	37 (30.8)
R.Chatram	2.S.Vadipatti	72 (100.0)	---	48 (66.7)	16 (22.2)	53 (73.6)	2 (2.8)	16 (22.2)
Dindigul	3.Chatrapatti	55 (93.0)	4 (7.0)	9 (16.3)	23 (41.8)	46 (83.6)	4 (7.2)	14 (25.4)
	Total (A)	247 (96.5)	9 (3.5)	84 (34.0)	83 (33.6)	203 (82.2)	23 (9.3)	67 (27.1)
	Underdeveloped							
Athoor	1.Indirapuram	43 (84.3)	8 (15.7)	19 (44.1)	9 (20.9)	20 (46.5)	6 (13.9)	8 (18.6)
R.Chatram	2.Kathiriyankulam	55 (100.0)	---	15 (27.2)	17 (30.9)	32 (58.1)	5 (9.0)	14 (25.4)
Dindigul	3.Kiriyampatti	53 (100.0)	---	20 (37.7)	20 (37.7)	36 (67.9)	6 (11.3)	13 (24.5)
	Total (B)	151 (95.0)	8 (5.0)	54 (35.8)	46 (30.5)	88 (58.3)	17 (11.2)	35 (23.2)
	Grand Total (A+B)	398 (95.9)	17 (4.1)	138 (34.7)	129 (32.4)	291 (73.1)	40 (10.0)	102 (25.6)

Source: Computed from primary data * Figures in parantheses indicate percentages (Multiple responses)

1. Obtaining employment, 2. take care of Children, 3. Sharing family expenditure, 4. Taking to workspot, 5. Carryout household work.

Group-wise, the incidence of not caring for their sick wives is more among the husbands of underdeveloped villages (30.2 per cent) than among the husbands of developed villages (23.4 per cent).

The responses show that in the study area the traditional habit of mutual help between husband and wife and interpersonal relationship among the family members still persist without any change. These are the main, assets of rural India.

It is a well known fact that a family comes up well only by the joint responsibility of husband and wife. Table 5.41 reveals the details of getting support from husbands to carry out the household activities by the women labourers. The respondents of this study were asked whether they get any support from their husbands. Of the 415 respondents living with their husbands, the majority (95.9 per cent) reported that they get support from their husbands while the remaining 4.1 per cent did not get it.

Regarding the type of support, nearly three-fourths (73.1 per cent) stated that their husbands support the family by sharing the family expenditure. The husbands of 34.7 per cent search for and obtain employment for their wives while one-third of the husbands (32.4 per cent) take care of their children. Sharing the household activities is a type of support received by one-fourth of the respondents (25.6 per cent) and 10 per cent reported that their husbands take them to the workplace.

There were more number of women labourers from the developed villages (96.5 per cent) who reported to receive some type of support from their husbands. Sharing the family expenditure (82.2 per cent) and sharing the household activities (27.1 per cent) were the major types of support in the developed villages, whereas obtaining employment (35.8 per cent), taking care of children (30.5 per cent) and taking their wives to work-spot (11.2 per cent) were the major supports received by more women labourers of the underdeveloped villages.

Sharing the family expenditure, searching for and getting employment for wives, taking care of children, sharing the household activities were the major types of support received by the majority of the respondents from their husbands. It is inferred that the majority of the husbands are conscious of their family responsibility and are ready to help their wives in running the family smoothly.

Sometimes the womenfolk are expected to go for work regularly and, whenever these women do not go for work for some reasons, their husbands do not accept it. There are a few husbands who understand the problem and accept it positively. Table 5.42 shows the husbands' reaction when the women labourers did not go for work. The women labourers of this study were also requested to express the reaction of their husbands when they (wives) stayed back in the home. Of the 415 respondents living with their husbands, nine-tenths (89.8 per cent) expressed that their husbands accepted the conditions, while another 6.3 per cent do not accept but do not react negatively, in the case of the remaining 3.9 per cent, the husbands get angry and scold their wives for not going to work.

Group-wise, there is not much difference in the case of accepting and not accepting by their husbands. But in the case of their husbands getting angry, 7.5 per cent of the women labourers from underdeveloped villages are suffering a lot.

The majority of the women labourers (89.8 per cent) stated that their husbands do not show any negative reactions but accept and understand the problems when they do not go for work for various reasons.

Treatment by Other Members in Family

In most of the cases the workers used to go in groups to their working place. The women labourers of this study also used to accompany others to their workspot. When asked with whom they go to the workplace they have given a number of answers. Table 5.43 depicts the people accompanying the women labourers to their workplaces.

Table 5.42. Treatment by Husband for not Going for Work

Block	Village	Accept	Donot Accept	Becomes Angry	Total
	Developed				
Athoor	1. Athoor	121 (96.8)	4 (3.2)	---	125
R.Chatram	2. S.Vadipatti	65 (90.2)	4 (5.6)	3 (4.2)	72
Dindigul	3. Chatrapatti	48 (81.4)	10 (16.9)	1 (1.7)	59
	Total (A)	234 (91.4)	18 (7.0)	4 (1.6)	256 (61.7)
	Underdeveloped				
Athoor	1. Indirapuram	43 (84.3)	5 (9.8)	3 (5.9)	51
R.Chatram	2. Kathiriyankulam	49 (89.0)	3 (5.5)	3 (5.5)	55
Dindigul	3. Kiriyampatti	47 (88.7)	--	6 (11.3)	53
	Total (B)	139 (87.5)	8 (5.0)	12 (7.5)	159 (38.7)
	Grand Total (A+B)	373 (89.8)	26 (6.3)	16 (3.9)	415 (100.0)

Source: Computed from primary data

* Figures in parantheses indicate percentages (Multiple responses)

Table 5.43. Treatment by Husband for not Going for Work

Block	*Village*	*No Body*	*Husband*	*Relatives*	*Co-worker*	*Total*
	Developed					
Athoor	1. Athoor	21 (13.8)	8 (5.3)	62 (40.8)	125 (82.2)	152
R.Chatram	2. S.Vadipatti	11 (12.2)	3 (3.3)	36 (40.0)	65 (72.2)	90
Dindigul	3. Chatrapatti	14 (20.9)	1 (1.5)	2 (3.0)	50 (74.6)	67
	Total (A)	46 (14.9)	12 (3.9)	100 (32.4)	240 (77.7)	309 (61.8)
	Underdeveloped					
Athoor	1. Indirapuram	1 (1.5)	2 (3.1)	29 (44.6)	60 (92.3)	65
R.Chatram	2. Kathiriyankulam	5 (7.9)	---	16 (25.4)	59 (93.6)	63
Dindigul	3. Kiriyampatti	11 (17.5)	6 (9.5)	3 (4.7)	48 (76.2)	63
	Total (B)	17 (8 9)	8 (4.2)	48 (25.1)	167 (87.4)	191 (38.2)
	Grand Total (A+B)	63 (12.6)	20 (4.0)	148 (29.6)	407 (81.4)	500 (100.0)

Source: Computed from primary data

* Figures in parantheses indicate percentages (Multiple responses)

Among the total workers, 81.4 per cent of have reported that they go to the workspot along with their co-workers and another 29.6 per cent accompany their relatives. Another 12.6 per cent used to go alone whereas the remaining 4 per cent joined their husbands in going to the workplace.

Group-wise, 87.4 per cent of the women labourers from underdeveloped villages and 77.7 per cent from the developed villages go to the workspot with their co-workers; but 32.4 per cent from developed villages and 25.1 per cent from underdeveloped villages accompany their relatives. The incidence of going alone is more among the respondents of developed villages (14.9 per cent) than among the respondents of underdeveloped villages (8.9 per cent).

In many rural families, the women used to encourage their in-laws to go to work for various reasons and there are also cases of discouragement. The respondents, when enquired about their in-laws, have given interesting answers and they are presented in Table 5.44.

The majority of the respondents (85.6 per cent) were happy that their in-laws used to encourage them to go to work and only the remaining 14.4 per cent were discouraged. As for the reasons for encouragement their employment helps to share the family expenditure (84.0 per cent), helps to meet debts (76.8 per cent) and it helps to save and to create assets, as reported by (22.4 per cent).

The reasons for discouragement included neglect of children (38.1 per cent) and neglect of household work (71.4 per cent). The support activities by the in-laws included house maintenance (52.0 per cent), child rearing (52.0 per cent), kitchen work (55.5 per cent), washing (41.7 per cent) and collecting water and fire wood (61.6 per cent).

Group-wise, women labourers of both the category of villages have got encouragement from their in-laws to go to work for the reasons as stated.

Table 5.44. Encouragement by In-laws to go to Work and Getting Support to Carryout Household Activities

Block	Village	No.of Respondents have inlaws	Encouragement	Discour-agement	Reasons for Encouragement		
					1	2	3
	Developed						
Athoor	1. Athoor	34	31 (91.2)	3 (8.8)	31 (100.0)	25 (80.6)	15 (48.4)
R.Chatram	2. S.Vadipatti	25	19 (76.0)	6 (24.0)	14 (73.7)	13 (68.4)	2 (10.5)
Dindigul	3. Chatrapatti	17	14 (82.3)	3 (17.7)	12 (85.7)	7 (50.0)	2 (14.3)
	Total (A)	76 (52.0)	64 (84.2)	12 (15.8)	57 (89.1)	45 (70.3)	19 (29.7)
	Underdeveloped						
Athoor	1. Indirapuram	26	24 (92.3)	2 (7.7)	21 (87.5)	22 (91.7)	1 (4.2)
R.Chatram	2. Kathiriyankulam	23	20 (87.0)	3 (13.0)	16 (69.6)	19 (82.6)	7 (30.4)
Dindigul	3. Kiriyampatti	21	17 (81.0)	4 (19.0)	11 (64.7)	10 (58.8)	1 (5.9)
	Total (B)	70 (48.0)	61 (87.1)	9 (12.9)	48 (78.7)	51 (83.6)	9 (14.8)
	Grand Total (A+B)	146 (100.0)	125 (85.6)	21 (14.4)	105 (84.0)	96 (76.8)	28 (22.4)

Block	Village	Reasons for Discouragement		Supported Activities				
		a	b	c	d	e	f	g
	Developed							
Athoor	1. Athoor	1 (33.3)	2 (66.7)	21 (61.8)	22 (64.7)	24 (70.6)	19 (55.9)	21 (61.8)
R.Chatram	2. S.Vadipatti	1 (16.7)	5 (83.3)	8 (32.0)	11 (44.0)	5 (20.0)	5 (20.0)	10 (40.0)
Dindigul	3. Chatrapatti	2 (66.7)	2 (66.7)	8 (47.0)	2 (11.8)	8 (47.0)	6 (35.3)	8 (47.0)
	Total (A)	4 (33.3)	9 (75.0)	37 (48.7)	35 (46.1)	37 (48.7)	30 (39.5)	39 (51.3)
	Underdeveloped							
Athoor	1. Indirapuram	1 (50.0)	1 (50.0)	20 (77.0)	16 (61.5)	20 (77.0)	11 (42.3)	24 (92.3)
R.Chatram	2. Kathiriyankulam	1 (33.3)	3 (100.0)	11 (47.8)	21 (91.3)	14 (60.9)	12 (52.2)	16 (69.5)
Dindigul	3. Kiriyampatti	2 (50.0)	2 (50.0)	8 (38.1)	4 (19.0)	10 (47.6)	8 (38.1)	11 (52.4)
	Total (B)	4 (44.4)	6 (66.6)	39 (55.7)	41 (58.6)	44 (62.9)	31 (44.3)	51 (72.3)
	Grand Total (A+B)	8 (38.1)	15 (71.4)	76 (52.0)	76 (52.0)	81 (55.5)	61 (41.7)	90 (61.6)

Source: Computed from primary data * Figures in parantheses indicate percentages (Multiple responses)

1. Share the family expenditure, 2. Meet debt, 3. Creating saving/asset a. Neglect of children, b. Neglect of Household work, c. House maintenance, d. Child rearing, e. Kitchen work, f. Washing, g.Collecting and firewood

In the joint family system in rural areas, there is an occasional misunderstanding the in-laws and sometimes it leads to strained relationship. Table 5.45 shows the respondents recognition by and relationship with their in-laws. Among the 500 respondents only 146 (29.2 per cent) have in-laws in their families. These women labourers were asked whether their in-laws gave due recognition to them in taking decisions on important family matters. It is interesting to note that more than three-fourths (78.0 per cent) have answered positively and stated that their importance is recognised by their in-laws while taking decisions. The remaining 22.0 per cent felt sorry that they are not recognised but neglected by their in-laws.

Those respondents who were not recognised by their in-laws were further probed for the reasons for which 56.2 per cent have no idea. The remaining 43.8 per cent felt that they are neglected by their in-laws just because they are females.

The respondents were asked about their relationship with their in-laws and 69.2 per cent reported that they maintain only cordial relationship, whereas the remaining 30.8 per cent have only strained relationship with their in-laws.

Group-wise, 52 per cent of the women labourers from the developed villages and 48 per cent from the underdeveloped villages are living with their in laws. Recognition by in-laws is reported to be more in the developed villages (80.3 per cent) than in the underdeveloped villages (75.7 per cent).

With regard to the reasons for their being neglected, a higher percentage from the underdeveloped villages (41.7 per cent) have stated that they are neglected just because of their being females and this reason was expressed by 40 per cent of the women labourers from the developed villages. As for their relationship, a higher percentage of respondents from the developed villages (75.0 per cent) have cordial relationship with their in-laws, while only 62.8 per cent of those from the underdeveloped villages stated so.

Table 5.45. Recognition by the Relationship with In-Laws by Women Labourers

Block	Village	No. of Res. having in laws	Recognition in decision making		Reasons for neglecting		Relationship with in laws	
			Yes	No	No idea	Being Female	Cordial	Strained
	Developed							
Athoor	1. Athoor	34 (22.4)	30 (88.2)	4 (11.8)	2 (50.0)	2 (50.0)	25 (73.5)	9 (26.5)
R.Chatram	2. S.Vadipatti	25 (27.8)	22 (88.0)	3 (12.0)	2 (66.7)	1 (33.3)	20 (80.0)	5 (20.0)
Dindigul	3. Chatrapatti	17 (25.4)	9 (53.0)	8 (47.0)	5 (62.5)	3 (37.5)	12 (70.6)	5 (29.4)
	Total (A)	76 (52.0)	61 (80.3)	15 (19.7)	9 (60.0)	6 (40.0)	57 (75.0)	19 (25.0)
	Underdeveloped							
Athoor	1.Indirapuram	26 (40.0)	21 (80.8)	5 (19.2)	3 (60.0)	2 (40.0)	14 (53.8)	12 (46.2)
R.Chatram	2.Kathiriyankulam	23 (36.5)	20 (87.0)	3 (13.0)	---	3 (100.0)	15 (65.2)	8 (34.8)
Dindigul	3.Kiriyampatti	21 (33.3)	12 (57.1)	9 (42.9)	6 (66.7)	3 (33.3)	15 (71.4)	6 (28.6)
	Total (B)	70 (48.0)	53 (75.7)	17 (24.3)	9 (52.9)	8 (47.1)	44 (62.8)	26 (37.2)
	Grand Total (A+B)	146 (29.2)	114 (78.0)	32 (22.0)	18 (56.2)	14 (43.8)	101 (69.2)	45 (30.8)

Source: Computed from primary data

* Figures in parantheses indicate percentages (Multiple responses)

The fact that the majority of the women labourers (79 per cent) are given due respect and their importance is being recognised by their in-laws is a welcome trend, which indicates that the rural female workers are able to get their social status and equality in the family.

The family's economic burden is shared by women workers and their contribution (economically) may be a reason for the recognition. Further, 69.2 per cent of the women labourers maintain only cordial relationship with their in-laws and this shows their sense of responsibility and interest in the smooth functioning of the family.

Care and Education of Children

The majority of women labourers come from economically poor households. In most cases, the family income is not sufficient to meet the family expenses. This forces the women to earn and supplement their family income. If the women labourers have children, then they need some person to look after their children while they go to work. Table 5.46 shows the care of respondents' children during the working hours.

The women labourers were asked about the persons taking care of their children during the working hours. To this, 135 respondents (27.0 per cent) replied that they had children in the age group which needs day care. It was stated by 37.8 per cent of the women labourers that their husbands looked after their children. When probed further, they stated that their husbands got only seasonal employment and also some of them do not have sufficient work. So, they used to look after their children. The balwadi also (day care centres) play a major role in taking care of their children, as was stated by 28.9 per cent of the women labourers. The joint family system also helps in this aspect, where, the mothers-in-law of 25.2 per cent of the women labourers and the fathers-in-law of 23.0 per cent of the women labourers and the sisters-in-law of 15.5 per cent of the women labourers were involved in taking care of their children. The

Table 5.46. Care of Children during Working Hours

Block	Village	No. of Respondents	Father-in-law	Mother-in-law	Husband	Sister in-law	Own son/ daughter	Balwadi
	Developed							
Athoor	1. Athoor	45	5 (11.1)	8 (17.8)	26 (57.8)	14 (31.1)	13 (28.9)	5 (11.1)
R.Chatram	2. S.Vadipati	13	9 (69.2)	3 (23.0)	7 (53.8)	---	1 (7.7)	3 (23.0)
Dindigul	3. Chatrapati	25	3 (12.0)	3 (12.0)	12 (48.0)	1 (4.0)	4 (16.0)	4 (16.0)
	Total (A)	83 (61.5)	17 (20.5)	14 (16.8)	45 (54.2)	15 (18.1)	18 (21.7)	12 (14.4)
	Underdeveloped							
Athoor	1. Indirapuram	20	4 (20.0)	7 (35.0)	2 (10.0)	1 (5.0)	1 (5.0)	10 (50.0)
R.Chatram	2. Kathiriyankulam	15	8 (53.3)	9 (60.0)	2 (13.3)	2 (13.3)	2 (13.3)	4 (26.7)
Dindigul	3. Kiriyampatti	17	2 (11.7)	4 (23.5)	2 (11.7)	3 (17.6)	4 (23.5)	13 (76.4)
	Total (B)	52 (38.5)	14 (26.9)	20 (38.5)	6 (11.5)	6 (11.5)	7 (13.5)	27 (51.9)
	Grand Total (A+B)	135 (100.0)	31 (23.0)	34 (25.1)	51 (37.8)	21 (15.5)	25 (18.5)	39 (28.9)

Source: Computed from primary data

* Figures in parantheses indicate percentages (Multiple responses)

remaining 18.5 per cent of the respondents said that their elder sons and daughters took care of the children during the working hours.

The role of mothers-in-law and the balwadi are more significant in the underdeveloped villages, while the role of husbands is more in the developed villages. The mothers-in-law took the responsibility of caring for their children in the case of 38.5 per cent of the women labourers in underdeveloped villages; the percentage was 16.8 in the developed villages. The percentage of women labourers whose children were taken care of by the balwadis was high (51.9 per cent) in the underdeveloped villages as against only 14.4 per cent in the developed villages. The husbands of 54.2 per cent of the respondents in the developed villages took care of their children as against only 11.5 per cent of the husbands in the underdeveloped villages.

The husbands, since most of them do not get regular employment, look after their children in the case of 37.8 per cent. The day care centre (28.9 per cent) and the in-laws of the joint families also take care of the children of the women labourers during their working hours.

Thus the joint family system is a boon to the daughters-in-law and helps in many ways. The government must ensure the availability and proper functioning of day care centres in most of the villages.

Education is an important social resource and a means of reducing inequality in the society. It helps the individual to raise his social status in various ways. Knowledge, skills, values and attitudes acquired through education help one to lead a desired quality of life. Table 5.47 shows the women labourers' children's education and the reasons for not attending school.

There were a total of 486 children in the school going age group in the 500 families. Among these 486 children, 85.0 per cent were attending school and the remaining 15.0 per cent had discontinued their studies.

Table 5.47. Children's Education and Reasons for Dropout from School

Block	Village	Attending school	School dropout	Dropout class			Reasons for drop-out *		
				Primary	Secondary	Hr.Secondary	1	2	3
	Developed								
Athoor	1. Athoor	172	13	6 (46.1)	7 (53.9)	---	12 (92.9)	4 (3.1)	3 (2.3)
R.Chatram	2.S.Vadipatti	54	10	3 (30.0)	7 (70.0)	---	6 (60.0)	4 (40.0)	---
Dindigul	3.Chatrapatti	51	15	9 (60.0)	5 (33.3)	1 (6.7)	7 (46.7)	4 (26.7)	4 (26.7)
	Total (A)	277 (87.9)	38 (12.1)	18 (47.4)	19 (50.0)	1 (2.6)	25 (65.8)	12 (31.6)	7 (18.4)
	Underdeveloped								
Athoor	1. Indirapuram	40	13	9 (69.2)	4 (30.8)	---	7 (53.8)	7 (53.8)	2 (15.4)
R.Chatram	2. Kathiriyankulam	50	12	5 (41.7)	5 (41.7)	2 (16.6)	5 (41.7)	3 (25.0)	4 (33.3)
Dindigul	3. Kiriyampatti	46	10	8 (80.0)	1 (10.0)	1 (10.0)	8 (80.0)	3 (30.0)	2 (20.0)
	Total (B)	136 (79.5)	35 (20.5)	22 (62.9)	10 (28.6)	3 (8.5)	20 (57.1)	13 (37.1)	8 (22.9)
	Grand Total (A+B)	413 (85.0)	73 (15.0)	40 (54.8)	29 (39.7)	4 (5.5)	45 (61.6)	25 (34.2)	15 (20.5)

Source: Computed from primary data * Figures in parantheses indicate percentages (Multiple responses)

1. Poor Economic condition, 2. Not interested in studies, 3. Household work

Among the dropouts, 54.8 per cent had discontinued their studies at the primary school level whereas another 39.7 per cent went up to secondary school level. The remaining 5.5 per cent stopped their studies at the higher secondary level.

With regard to the reasons for their discontinuance of their studies, 61.6 per cent quoted their poor economic condition. Another 34.2 per cent were not interested in studies. Involvement in household activities was the reason stated by 20.5 per cent.

Group-wise, there were 12.1 per cent dropouts from the developed villages, a higher percentage of dropouts from the underdeveloped villages discontinued their studies at the primary level (62.9 per cent) and higher secondary level (8.5 per cent) whereas in the developed villages half of the dropouts (50.0 per cent) discontinued at the secondary level.

(iv) Level of Awareness about the Development Programmes

Development Programmes for Women Labourers

The governments (central and state) are implementing a number of development programmes for the welfare of various sections of the society, especially socially, economically and empowerment-wise weaker sections of the society. Women contribute substantially to the economic resources of a family both by way of services and wages. Yet development projects are meant mainly for men, while social welfare schemes cater mainly to women. However, an increasing realisation of the fact that women play an active role and have to be involved in rural development schemes is growing up. Therefore, it is necessary to know their level of awareness about the development schemes meant for development. Table 5.48 presents the women labourers awareness about the development programmes. Asked about their awareness about the development programmes, only 17.4 per cent of the respondents replied that they are aware of a few schemes and the rest (82.6 per cent) were not aware of any

Table 5.48. Awareness about Various Development Programmes of Government

Block	Village	No.of respondents		Awareness About			Sources		
		Total	Aware	IRDP	DWACRA	JRY	Relative	Neighbour	Govt. Officials
	Developed								
Athoor	1. Athoor	152	23 (15.1)	12 (7.9)	10 (6.6)	2 (1.3)	9 (5.9)	9 (5.9)	4 (2.6)
R.Chatram	2. S.Vadipatti	90	9 (10.0)	6 (6.7)	1 (1.1)	4 (4.4)	7 (7.8)	2 (2.27)	---
Dindigul	3. Chatrapatti	67	25 (37.3)	17 (25.4)	5 (7.4)	4 (6.0)	15 (22.4)	19 (28.3)	13 (19.4)
	Total (A)	309 (61.8)	57 (18.4)	35 (61.4)	16 (28.1)	10 (17.5)	31 (54.3)	30 (52.6)	17 (29.8)
	Underdeveloped								
Athoor	1. Indirapuram	65	10 (15.4)	5 (7.7)	4 (6.1)	1 (1.5)	5 (7.7)	10 (15.4)	---
R.Chatram	2. Kathiriyar kulam	63	6 (9.5)	4 (6.3)	---	3 (4.8)	2 (3.1)	21 (371.5)	3 (4.7)
Dindigul	3. Kiriyampatti	63	14 (22.2)	10 (32.0)	2 (3.2)	2 (3.2)	3 (4.7)	2 (3.2)	2 (3.3)
	Total (B)	191 (38.2)	30 (15.7)	19 (63.3)	6 (20.0)	6 (20.0)	20 (66.7)	12 (40.0)	5 (16.7)
	Grand Total (A+B)	500 (100.0)	87 (17.4)	54 (62.1)	22 (25.3)	16 (18.3)	51 (58.6)	42 (48.3)	22 (25.3)

Source: Computed from primary data * Figures in parantheses indicate percentages (Multiple responses)

Figure XII

Awareness about the Various Development Programmes of the Government by Women Labourers

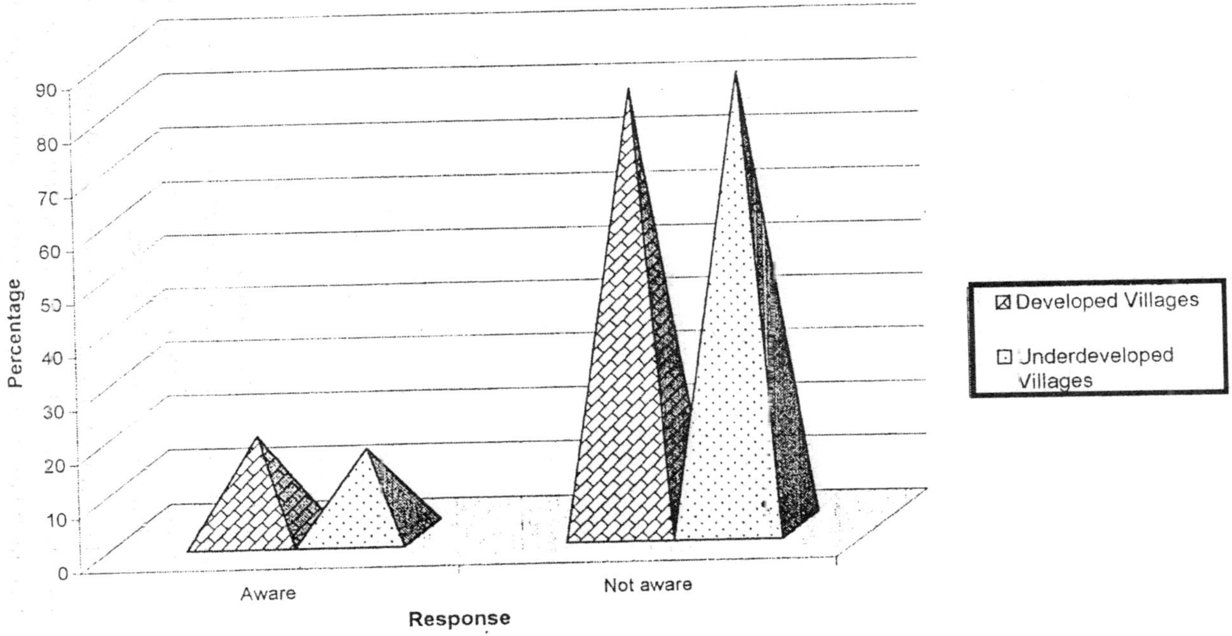

development programmes. Among those who were aware of some programmes, 62.1 per cent reported to be aware of the Integrated Rural Development Programme (IRDP), whereas another 25.3 per cent knew about the Development of Women and Children in Rural Areas (DWACRA) scheme. Jawahar Rozgar Yojana (JRY) was known to 18.3 per cent of the women labourers.

Group-wise, 18.4 per cent of the women labourers from the developed villages were aware of a few developmental programmes. IRDP (61.4 per cent) and JRY (17.5 per cent) were the programmes known to the majority women labourers from the developed villages whereas IRDP (66.3 per cent) is known to the women labourers of underdeveloped villages.

With regard to the sources of such awareness, 58.6 per cent of them knew of the schemes through their relatives. The neighbours have served as a source of information to 48.3 per cent of them while 25.3 per cent of them came to know with the help of governmental officials.

Relatives (66.7 per cent) from the underdeveloped villages neighbours and governmental officials (54.3 per cent and 29.8 per cent respectively from the developed villages) served as the major source of information to the women labourers.

Only 17.4 per cent of the respondents were aware of a few developmental programmes, like IRDP,DWACRA and JRY, which means that these women labourers have not been benefited by any development programmes of the government. In this context the district authorities should take efforts to disseminate Rural Development Information System so as to benefit the women-folk in the rural areas. In the recently introduced Gram Sabha meeting, the officials and elected representatives should inform the participants about the various schemes and programmes meant for rural areas in general and for women-folk in particular.

The Government has been introducing a number of measures for the betterment and improvement of the conditions of women labourers and taking different measures to solve the problems of these women labourers. The women labourers were asked about their opinion of the need for governmental intervention to solve their problems. Table 5.49 indicates the opinion of the women labourers about the need for governmental intervention to solve the problems of women labourers. The majority (61.6 per cent) of the women labourers stated that there is a need for government intervention to solve the problems of the women labourers whereas the remaining 38.4 per cent stated that there is no such need. That means that these women labourers are highly confident of solving their own problems.

Table 5.49 : Opinion Regarding Governmental Intervention to Solve Women Labour Problems

Block	*Village*	*Yes*	*No*	*Total*
	Developed			
Athoor	1. Athoor	92 (60.5)	60 (39.5)	152
R.Chatram	2. S.Vadipatti	58 (64.4)	32 (35.6)	90
Dindigul	3. Chatrapatti	39 (58.2)	28 (41.8)	67
	Total (A)	189 (61.2)	120 (38.8)	309 (61.8)
	Underdeveloped			
Athoor	1. Indirapuram	32 (49.2)	33 (50.8)	65
R.Chatram	2. Kathiriyankulam	60 (95.2)	3 (4.8)	63
Dindigul	3. Kiriyampatti	25 (39.7)	38 (60.3)	63
	Total (B)	119 (62.3)	72 (37.7)	191 (38.2)
	Grand Total (A+B)	308 (61.6)	192 (38.4)	500 (100.0)

Source: Computed from primary data * Figures in parantheses indicate percentages

Group-wise, a higher percentage of women labourers from the underdeveloped villages (62.3 per cent) felt the need for government intervention for solving their problems. The recent thoughts on women's rights and women empowerment have stimulated the women to find out various strategies to solve their own problems through mutual and co-operative efforts.

Government and other public bodies both at the centre and in the states have committed themselves to socio-economic development of the women-folk. Their obligations have been made explicit through plans and programmes to improve the employment level and income status of the women folk. It is evident from the field level data that the majority of the landless women labourers belong to the lower strata and they expect more from governments and non-governmental organisations. Table 5.50 shows the expectations of the women labourers from the GOs and NGOs.

The women labourers were asked to spell out their expectations from Government and Non-Government Organisations. It is noted that the percentage of women labourers expecting benefits from NGOs is higher than those expecting from GOs. From the government side a little less than one-fifth of the women labourers (18.6 per cent) wanted financial assistance for their upliftment, 13.2 per cent needed medical aid; insurance facilities for their life was the demand of 10.2 per cent of the women labourers; and 5.6 per cent required accident benefits.

Group-wise, the number of respondents demanding financial help was more (21.4 per cent) in the developed villages. The other three types of benefits were also demanded by more number of persons from the developed villages.

With regard to their expectations from the NGOs, regular employment chances was given topmost priority by more than half of the women labourers (55.0 per cent). The other types of expectations included facilities for education of their children (43.4 per cent), medical aid free of cost (36.6 per cent), creating awareness about their rights (35.4 per cent) and financial help (15.4 per cent).

Table 5.50. Expectations from GOs and NGOs for Development of Women Labourers

Block	Village	No.of Respondents	Government					Non-Govt. Organisations			
			1	2	3	4	5	6	7	8	9
	Developed										
Athoor	1. Athoor	152	10 (6.6)	7 (4.6)	16 (10.5)	21 (13.8)	1 (6.5)	93 (62.2)	125 (82.2)	114 (75.0)	92 (60.5)
R.Chatram	2.S.Vadipatti	90	23 (25.6)	20 (22.2)	24 (26.7)	21 (23.3)	18 (20.0)	68 (75.6)	32 (35.6)	29 (32.2)	24 (26.7)
Dindigul	3.Chatrapatti	67	7 (10.4)	6 (8.9)	26 (38.8)	16 (23.4)	4 (5.8)	23 (34.3)	15 (22.4)	10 (14.9)	10 (14.9)
	Total (A)	309 (61.8)	40 (12.9)	33 (10.7)	66 (21.4)	58 (18.8)	23 (7.4)	184 (59.5)	172 (55.7)	153 (49.5)	126 (40.8)
	Underdeveloped										
Athoor	1.Indirapuram	65	28 (43.1)	14 (21.5)	13 (20.0)	1 (1.5)	1 (1.5)	29 (44.6)	32 (49.2)	15 (23.1)	19 (29.2)
R.Chatram	2.Kathiriyankulam	63	1 (1.6)	2 (3.2)	11 (17.5)	3 (4.8)	1 (1.6)	48 (76.1)	6 (9.5)	6 (9.5)	29 (46.0)
Dindigul	3.Kiriyampatti	63	8 (12.6)	2 (3.2)	3 (4.8)	4 (6.3)	1 (1.6)	16 (22.2)	7 (11.1)	3 (4.8)	9 (14.3)
	Total (B)	191 (38.2)	37 (19.4)	18 (9.4)	27 (14.1)	8 (4.2)	5 (2.6)	91 (47.6)	45 (23.6)	24 (12.6)	57 (29.8)
	Grand Total (A+B)	500 (100.0)	77 (15.4)	51 (10.2)	93 (18.6)	66 (13.2)	28 (5.6)	275 (55.0)	217 (43.4)	177 (34.0)	183 (36.6)

Source: Computed from primary data * Figures in parantheses indicate percentages (Multiple responses)

1. Financial help, 2. Insurance, 3. Finance Assistance, 4. Medical aid, 5. Accidential benefit, 6. Employment, 7. Edn. of Children, 8. Rights and Power, 9. Medical aid.

Group-wise, except financial help, which was demanded by a higher percentage of women labourers (19.4 per cent) from the underdeveloped villages, all the other requirements were expected by more number of women labourers from the developed villages.

The people expect the services of the NGOs more than those of the GOs and this may be due to the reasons such as the non-helping attitude of the government officials. The study reveals that the people expect more from the NGOs than from the GOs.

From the government side, they expect financial assistance (in the form of loans or subsidies or trees), medical aid etc. But from the NGOs side, they demand employment chances, education for their children, free medical aid, and creating awareness about their rights. Further NGOs and GOs should come forward to provide skill formation to the women labourers so as to improve their human capital which can be productively employed for development of rural areas.

Usually the labourers can join the unions with some expectations and the unions have a certain role to play for the welfare of the labourers. Table 5.51 shows the expected role of union/association as per the women labourers. None of these 500 respondents were members of any union. They were asked about the role the union or association has to play. To this, two-thirds of them (66.4 per cent) stated that the unions should help to get a higher wage from the employer. Another 41.0 per cent were not able to specifically mention the role of unions but reported generally that the unions should help the labourers to get more benefits from the employers. Help to get more awareness about their working environment, rights and privileges was role of the union as expressed by 13.2 per cent.

Group-wise, help to get more wages was the major role expressed by 68.1 per cent of the women labourers from underdeveloped villages, whereas help to get more benefits (49.5 per cent) and creating awareness (16.2 per cent) were the roles

Table 5.51. Expectations of Women Labourers from Trade Union/Association

Block	*Village*	*Total No.of Respondents*	*To get more wage*	*More benefits*	*To get more awareness*
	Developed				
Athoor	1. Athoor	152	91 (59.9)	79 (52.0)	39 (25.7)
R.Chatram	2.S.Vadipatti	90	60 (66.7)	60 (66.7)	9 (10.0)
Dindigul	3.Chatrapatti	67	51 (14.9)	14 (20.9)	2 (2.9)
	Total (A)	309 (61.8)	202 (65.4)	153 (49.5)	50 (16.2)
	Underdeveloped				
Athoor	1.Indirapuram	65	41 (63.0)	4 (6.1)	1 (1.5)
R.Chatram	2.Kathiriyankulam	63	44 (69.8)	28 (44.4)	---
Dindigul	3.Kiriyampatti	63	45 (71.4)	20 (31.7)	15 (23.8)
	Total (B)	191 (38.2)	130 (68.1)	52 (27.2)	16 (8.4)
	Grand Total (A+B)	500 (100.0)	332 (66.4)	205 (41.0)	66 (13.2)

Source: Computed from primary data

* Figures in parantheses indicate percentages (Multiple responses)

6

Summary, Major Findings, Suggestions and Conclusion

Introduction

A brief summary of the study, its major findings and suggestions are presented in this last chapter. Women constitute half of the population and their development reflects the progress of society. The status of women in society is measured in terms of their level of income, employment, education, health as well as the role played by them in family, community and society. Women are a vital and productive work force in India's economy. In 1999 UNDP ranked India in the last quartile of the countries (112 out of 143 countries) in a gender - related development index (GDI).Women labour in rural India are involved in a variety of occupations like agriculture and allied activities, construction, plantation, beedi rolling, brick kiln, leather tanneries, mill work and other work.

Due to their lower socio-economic status, women are not only ill represented in different walks of life, but are also subjected to various forms of socio-economic and sexual violence. This is more among women labourers, particularly landless labourers belonging generally to the Scheduled Caste community. The economic vulnerability of the family compels their women to go to work, supplementing the income of their respective families. Being illiterates and unskilled, they are forced to work under harsh and deplorable working environments. The problem is more acute among the rural landless women labourers. These rural landless woman labourer is victimized in three ways: (i) as a woman she is dominated by men; (ii) as a worker she is exploited and therefore she earns low wages; and, (iii) as a member of a particular caste she is kept only at a particular level of social order. Women are generally outside the reach of laws and governmental schemes that seek to protect their social security and improve their working conditions.

Statement of the Problem

Women labour is an important segment of the total workforce in India. According to the census of 1991, more than 90 per cent of the working women are engaged as wage labourers in the unorganised sector. Although, Indian society has completed five decades of development planning, very little change can be found in the status of the women force in our country. Most of the women, when compared with men, bear the brunt of poverty and they are also very often subject to different kinds of discrimination and exploitation.

Women workers constitute a large chunk (Census 1991) of agricultural labour in India. The social status of women labourers reveals that most of them belong to socially backward and economically disadvantaged groups.

Women participate in economically productive activities outside the home. The size of female population and female work force in India indicates the potential strength of women in the human resources of the country. The women labourers, particularly the rural landless ones, suffer from social disabilities and are prone to continuous exploitation. Their living conditions are very poor and their earnings are very low and are not sufficient for their subsistence.

In the light of the above, it is necessary to study the prevailing socio-economic status of women, their problems in the work environment and problems of equation with their husbands and in-laws in the home. This kind of study will enable the researcher to suggest ways and means to promote the welfare of the rural landless women labourers. Hence this study.

Title of the Study

"Problems of Rural Landless Women Labourers in Dindigul District".

Objectives

The objectives of the present study are:

1. to study the present socio-economic status of landless women labourers belonging to farm and non-farm sectors in developed and underdeveloped villages in the study area;
2. to find out the problems faced by them in their work environment;
3. to examine the major problems faced by them in home management;
4. to understand the degree and level of awareness about the development programmes among the landless women labourers; and,
5. to suggest ways and means to promote the welfare of the landless women labourers.

Methodology

This is an explorative study of descriptive nature. Survey method has been used in this study with the help of a pre-tested interview schedule specially designed for collecting comprehensive information for fulfilling the objectives of the study.

Area and Sample for the Study

The study was conducted in six villages of Dindigul District. This district was selected for the study in view of the availability of various landless labourers involved in different occupations.

Dindigul District has 14 development blocks. Multi-stage purposive sampling method was adopted for selection of respondents. Among 6 taluks of Dindigul District only one Dindigul Taluk, was selected at the first stage. Among the four blocks of Dindigul Taluk, Shanarpatty Block was used for the pre-test and the remaining three (Athoor, Reddiarchatram and Dindigul) blocks were used for the actual study purpose in the second stage. The third stage consisted of selecting the six villages at the rate of two villages per block. In each block two villages, viz one developed village and one underdeveloped village were selected. Developed and underdeveloped villages were identified on the basis of irrigation and infrastructural facilities. The study respondents were selected at the fourth stage of the sampling procedure. With regard to respondents census method covered all the landless women labourers who were identified with the help of balwadi teachers and mahalir mandrams (women's clubs) in the selected villages.

Data Collection

Relevant and required data for the present study have been collected from primary and secondary sources. The secondary data on district, taluk, blocks and villages were collected from both published and unpublished sources. The required primary data for the present study were collected from the landless women labourers. For this purpose, a well planned and structured interview schedule was prepared in consultation with experts working in this field. Since the majority of the landless women labourers were illiterate, it was decided to apply the interview schedule as a tool of data collection and the schedule was prepared in their mother tongue (Tamil).

The interview schedule prepared was administered for pre-test to a sample of 50 women labourers in the Shanarpatty block. The pre-test helped the researcher to modify, revise and finalise the schedule. Apart from the interview schedule, the researcher also made field observation to understand the work and home environment. Further, the researcher has held focussed group discussions with the women labourers in each village. Thus, interview schedule, field observation and focussed group discussion were used as the techniques for collection of primary data for this study.

For analysing the data, percentage and simple average methods were used. The data were coherently presented in tables, diagrams and charts for analysis and discussion.

Scope of the Study

It is an empirical study at the grass root level and the study will focus on different types of problems encountered by the women labourers in developed as well as underdeveloped villages. It can guide the district and state level officials in formulating policies and programmes for the welfare of the women labourers. It can be useful to the voluntary organisations who are already involved in implementing welfare programmes for women and women labour, especially the poor landless women labourers. This can help other researchers to take up further research work on empowerment of rural women and women labourers.

Constraints

The study was confined to six selected villages in a district as a micro level study even though the results can be generalised for the whole of Tamil Nadu at the macro level.

For collecting necessary data from the field source, interview, field observation and focussed group discussions were used as tools. In the focussed group discussions and the interview there could be some recall bias.

Major Findings

The important findings of the present study are classified into four broad areas as shown hereunder.

I. Socio-economic background of the landless women labourers in the study area

1. The majority (61.8 per cent) of the women labourers were from the developed villages, because of the greater concentration of landless labour families in these villages.

2. The majority (62.3 per cent) of the women labourers were in the age group of 20-39 years. It shows that the women are forced to share the family responsibilities at a young age. This may be the reason for their lack of awareness about their rights and privileges.

3. The majority (83 per cent) of the women labourers were married. It reveals that the Indian women are allowed to work outside the home after their marriage because they belong to poor families.

4. Regarding educational status, 69 per cent were illiterates which is below the Tamil Nadu State literacy rate of 62.66 and the national literacy rate of 52.1 per cent (Census 1991). The underdeveloped villages have more number of illiterates and it is due to lack of educational institutions. This may be the reason for their lack of awareness about their rights and privileges.

5. With regard to occupation, the majority (91.4 per cent) were agricultural labourers, and the number was high in the developed villages due to the availability of more irrigated areas providing more employment chances to the women labourers. Further, only 12.4 per cent of the women labourers had subsidiary occupations like agricultural labour, construction work, brick work, board mill work and basket-making. This should be increased to help women labourers to earn more during the off-season. In the underdeveloped villages more number of women labourers were involved in brick kiln work. Here the availability of employment chances in agricultural activity was less and hence they had to go in for non-agricultural activities.

6. Caste plays a major role in the social stratification in Indian rural society and it is more so in rural areas. The Scheduled Caste women labourers formed the majority (72 per cent) in the study villages. There were 77.5 per cent SC women labourers from the underdeveloped villages and 68.6 per cent from the developed villages. This shows that the Scheduled Caste people of these study villages must be guided and helped both economically and employment wise to come up in their life.

7. The women labourers, the majority (86.6 per cent) of the women labourers came from nuclear families. Group-wise, the percentage of nuclear families was high (87.7 per cent) in the developed villages and the percentage of joint families was high (16 per cent) in the underdeveloped villages.

8. Nearly 44 per cent of the family members from the underdeveloped villages were illiterates. This is because these villages do not have adequate educational facilities. Further the percentage of low-level educated persons (primary level, 24.3 per cent) was high in the underdeveloped villages when compared to the developed villages. To reduce the illiteracy rate the government should take necessary measures by establishing more schools in the remote villages and to motivate parents to send their children to schools instead of sending them to work.

9. The majority of family members (74 per cent) were involved in agriculture and allied activities. It is more in developed villages (81 per cent) and the reason is that the irrigation facilities assured more scope for employment in the field of agriculture.

10. The monthly income of the majority of the women labourers' (62 per cent) families was between Rs.1000 and 2000. Group-wise, the income was is higher in underdeveloped villages because the respondent families from these villages were engaged in non-farm activities that gave them a higher income. So, the government and non-government organisations may augment non-farm activities in rural

areas, thereby increasing the income of women labourers in the study area.

11. The majority (67 per cent) of the women labourer families spent Rs.1001 to Rs.2000 per month. The families that spent less than Rs.1000 per month are more in developed villages than in underdeveloped villages. It is mainly due to their dependence only on agricultural activities as well as that they need not spend much on extra items like transport since they work only in and around their villages.

12. With regard to housing condition of the women labourers, 83 per cent of them have houses of their own. Nearly half of the women labourers live in thatched type of houses, while 64.8 per cent of the houses were tiled. With reference to the condition, 59.4 per cent of the houses were moderate. This clearly indicates the poor economic status of the women labourers and that the low income earned by them could not meet their daily needs. Due to this situation, it is very difficult for the women labourers to repair their houses which are in dilapidated condition.

13. Nearly half (49.4 per cent) of the women labourer families own assets to the value of less than Rs.10.000. The families from the underdeveloped villages own assets of a higher value than the families of the developed villages. It is due to the higher earnings of labourers involved non-farm activities like mill work, brick kiln work and other work. Whereas in developed villages the labourers are only dependent upon agriculture, which is normally low paid work.

14. With regard to monetary debt of the women labourer families, 39 per cent of them have borrowed money (57 per cent from developed and 43 per cent from underdeveloped villages) for various purposes like meeting family expenses, constructing houses and purchase of milch animals etc.

15. Among the borrowers 43 per cent have borrowed less than Rs. 2500. If regular employment opportunities are available

provided in non-farm occupations, it will increase their earnings and they will not borrow money in future.

16. Moneylenders (62.4 per cent) played a major role in providing loans to the women labourer families and institutional sources like banks and cooperatives societies contributed very little (1.8 per cent). This indicates the urgent need to provide institutional credit to the women labourers and also curtail the role of village moneylenders.

17. With regard to income share of the women known to total family income, the majority (57.6 per cent) of the women labourers contribute 25-49 per cent of their family income. The share of income (25-49 per cent) of the women labourers is high in underdeveloped villages (59.2 per cent) than in developed villages (57 per cent). This indicates that the earnings of the women labourers of underdeveloped villages is comparatively high because they engaged in non-farm work. To increase the income of the labourers the government should encourage and initiate non-farm activities in rural areas.

18. The proportion of expenditure on food was 50-74 per cent of total expenditure in the case of 60 per cent of the women labourer families. This means that three-fourths of the family expenditure was on food, resulting in deficit of money for other expenses and there could be no saving. This practice of money spending is more among the families of underdeveloped villages.

II. Problems Faced by the Women Labourers in the Work Environment

19. The majority (93 per cent) of the women labourers worked within the village. The majority of the women labourers were involved agriculture and allied activities both within and outside the village area.

20. The majority of the women (94.6 per cent) used to go on foot to work. The use of public transport facilities (23.2 per cent)

was more among the women labourers from the underdeveloped villages, since they had to go a long distance to work in the mills.

21. The reasons for choosing their present occupation were non-availability of any other work (60.6 per cent) and availability of this work within the village (55.0 per cent). This shows that they do not want to depend only upon agriculture but they want to find some employment opportunities to support their family income and hence they have no other alternative except to agree to choose any employment available.

22. The majority of the agricultural labourers (78.8 per cent) and 60.5 per cent of the non-farm labourers reported to work for 10-20 days in a month. They are unemployed for the remaining 10 days in a month. This shows that the labourers search for alternative work for their unemployed days.

23. In case of subsidiary occupations, 80 per cent of the agricultural and 67.6 per cent of the non-agricultural labourers got work for less than 10 days in a month. This shows that the women labourers should have subsidiary occupations like rearing of milch animal, doing petty business and other work in rural areas. The government should implement employment oriented development programmes, especially skill development and development of entrepreneurial skill. This will enhance their income. Poor rain fall (75.2 per cent), poor employment opportunities (62.2 per cent), seasonal occupation (22.0 per cent) were reported to be the major reasons for unemployment among the women labourers. Group-wise, only 70.9 per cent of those from the developed villages expressed poor rainfall because these villages have better irrigation facilities than the underdeveloped villages with only rainfed area. Hence a higher percentage (82.2 per cent) of the latter attributed poor rainfall as a major reason for unemployment in their villages. The government can ensure proper irrigation facility

to increase the area under cultivation. In turn it will promote employment opportunities. Further, the government should organise training programmes in non-farm activities, to promote employment generation during off-season.

24. In the study villages, the male (89.8 per cent) labourers got Rs. 26-90 per day as his wage depending upon the nature of his work. For women (92.0 per cent), the wage rate was Rs.25. Group-wise, the female (17.3 per cent) got Rs. 26-50 from the underdeveloped villages because of non-farm work. Therefore, to increase the income of women labourers, the government should give training in non-farm activities and steps must be taken to enforce minimum wages and equal remuneration for equal work.

25. The majority (83.8 per cent) of the women labourers received daily wages. This shows the temporary nature of the work. More number of (23 per cent) women labourers from the underdeveloped villages got their wages weekly because these labourers used to work mainly in mills.

26. Nearly 30.0 per cent of the women labourers face problems in getting their wages after work. The major types of problems are overtime work without any additional wages (54.5 per cent), delay in payment of wages (22.7 per cent), have to wait for a longer time to receive wages (10.3 per cent) and the demand for commission by the agents and contractors (10.3 per cent). These types of problems are present both in developed (30.1 per cent) and underdeveloped villages (28.3 per cent). These types of exploitation are more among the agricultural labourers because of its unorganised nature and basically they are illiterates lacking in skill and so they have low bargaining power.

27. Only 11 per cent of the women labourers enjoy some facilities like day care centre, first aid facilities, rest room, toilet, canteen and creche in their workspot. This shows that the workers in the unorganised sector need to be given basic facilities in their workspot.

28. The majority of the women labourers (90.8 per cent) were not aware of the fixed working hours as per government rule. This may be because of their illiteracy and their negligence to know the rules and also there is nobody to educate them about this. Also, as this is an unorganised sector, no trade union involvement is seen and this may also be one of the reasons.

29. As for the maximum hours they work, the majority (64.4 per cent) used to work for 7-8 hours a day and nearly 15 per cent work 8-9 hours. Also more than three-fourths (34 per cent) of them work for more than 8 hours per day. This needs to be looked into and this may be due to their ignorance and hence, the employers try to exploit their labour.

30. With regard to the number of days worked more than the specified working hours, 73 per cent of them work overtime for 10 days in a month. Among the overtime workers, 51.5 per cent used to get Rs. 6-10 per day for the extra work done. This shows that the women labourers were not able to get their due wage for the extra work done, because of the absence of organisation to protect their rights. It is a crying need to form women's labour unions or organisations to safeguard and promote their welfare.

31. It is really a sorry state of affairs that only eight women labourers out of the total were aware of the Minimum Wages Act. This necessitates to create awareness among the women labourers about the Minimum Wages Act and the various provisions and facilities for the labourers. The majority of the women labourers (89 per cent) receive their wages directly from their employers.

III. Problems Faced by the Women Labourers in Home Management

32. The husbands of the majority of the women labourers (97.1 per cent) have accepted and permitted their wives to work. This attitude of husbands towards permitting their wives

to work and earn is a good sign of development. The reasons for their acceptance includes additional income for the family (72 per cent) and sharing family expenditure (50 per cent). The reasons for not permitting by their husbands are low rate of wage and requiring more hard work. Thus, women labourers in the study area directly help in enhancing the economic status of the family.

33. The majority (90.1 per cent) of the women labourers' husbands were satisfied with the working hours of the respondents. Those women labourers whose husbands were not satisfied with the working hours have stated the reasons for their dissatisfaction as the working time is same for both the husbands and wife, long hours of work and child care not possible.

34. The husbands of the majority (91.6 per cent) of the women labourers were satisfied with the present wage of their wives. The reasons for dissatisfaction were insufficient wage and the wages are not proportionate to their work. The government should take necessary steps to increase the wages and to give appropriate skill training to the women labourers and it will increase their earning capacity.

35. The majority (79.3 per cent) of the women labourers were able to get the entire earnings of their husbands for the family. Spending on alcohol and smoking are the major types of unnecessary and unhealthy expenses which prevented some husbands from surrendering their entire earnings to the family. So, steps must be taken to create awareness about the evil effect of alcoholism and smoking.

36. With regard to the expenditure incurred on these habits nearly one-third (30.8 per cent) of the husbands spent more than Rs. 200 per month and their number is more from the underdeveloped villages. The government and non-governmental agencies should create awareness about the evil of these unhealthy habits and conduct programmes to change the behaviour of these husbands, so that they can

avoid these habits. Thereby they will be able to create a peaceful environment in their family.

37. Only 11 per cent of the women labourers work with their husbands. The majority (57.4 per cent) of those working with their husbands stated sharing of work among them and security to the women worker as the advantages enjoyed by them. Even though there are advantages in working with their husbands, they could not always get employment chances for both of them in the same place.

38. As for problems with husbands faced by the women labourers, 27.6 per cent of the women labourers faced some problems. Addiction to alcohol and smoking and petty quarrels were the major type of problems. These problems were more in the underdeveloped villages and these problems resulted in waste of money. They also affected the health. It is the necessary to take steps to save the husbands of these women labourers from the clutches of evil alcoholism and promote the saving habit through organisation of self-help groups in the study area.

39. The study shows that 75.6 per cent of the women labourers were consulted in the decision making process by their husbands and that they are given due recognition. This recognition and involvement is mainly due to their share in economic activities of the family. The women still need to be given due respect and should be consulted on all matters. There are a considerable (24 per cent) number of women without knowing the adequate reason for their not being consulted. This pathetic condition should be changed by providing proper awareness about their role, rights and responsibilities in the family.

40. The majority (74 per cent) of husbands rendered assistance to their wives during illness. The type of help included taking the wife to the hospital, providing medicine during illness, sharing family work etc. This shows that the relationship between husband and wife is mutual and this

relationship still persists without any change in the study area. The modes of non-assistance by the husbands included neglecting them during illness and illitreating them in an alcoholic mood. This behaviour should be changed through counselling programmes for these husbands to change their behaviour and to make them realise the importance of better environment in the family.

41. The majority of (96 per cent) of the women labourers got support from their husbands in household activities. The major types of support included sharing family expenditure, sharing the household activities, searching and getting employment for wives, and taking care of children. This shows that the majority of the husbands are ready to help their wives in running the family smoothly.

42. The majority (89.8 per cent) of the husbands did not show any negative reactions when their wives did not go to work but accepted and understood the problems when their wives did not go for work for various reasons. But a few of them got angry and scolded their wives for not going to work. This may be due to their poor economic condition and because their earning is very much needed for their survival.

43. The majority of (85.6 per cent) the women labourers' in-laws used to encourage them to go to work and the reasons for their encouragement included to share the family expenditure, helps to meet debts and helps to save and to create assets. The reasons for discouragement included neglect of children and neglect of household work.

44. The supportive activities of the in-laws included house maintenance, child rearing, kitchen work, washing and collecting water and firewood. This shows that the majority of the women labourers were encouraged and supported by their in-laws. This cooperation helps the existence of the joint family system in the villages.

45. The majority of (78.0 per cent) the women labourers were given due respect and their importance was being recognized

by their in-laws. This shows the rural women workers able to get their social status and equality in the family. This is due to the women workers' share in the family income. Further, 69 per cent of the women labourers maintained cordial relationship with their in-laws. This indicates that the women labourers' income in the family helps to enhance their status and recognition in the family.

46. Only 27 per cent of the women labourers had children in the age group which needed day care. The persons taking care of their children included husbands (37.8 per cent), day care centre (29 per cent), and the in-laws in the joint families. This shows that the women labourers should be provided with sufficient day care centres to look after their children. The government should take necessary step to increase the number of day care centres in the study area.

47. The majority (85 per cent) of the children of the women labourers were attending school and the remaining (15 per cent) per cent discontinued their studies. Among the dropouts 54.8 per cent discontinued their studies at the primary school level and another 40 per cent at the secondary school level. Group-wise the dropout rate at the primary school level is high (62 per cent) in the underdeveloped villages. This may be due to absense of school facilities in the villages itself. The major reason for discontinuing their education were poor economic condition, not interested in studies and involvement in household activities in both types of villages. This indicates the urgent need to create awareness about the importance of education among the women labourers in the study area. The non-government agencies should organise awareness camps in the study area and also education facilities should be provided in the village itself.

IV. Awareness about the Various Development Programmes

48. Only 17.4 per cent of the women labourers were aware of a few developmental programmes like IRDP, DWCRA, and JRY, which means that these women labourers have not

been benefited by any development programmes of the government. The government and non-government agencies should take necessary efforts to make the women labourers aware of the various women development programmes and other rural development programmes by conducting special awareness camps in rural areas. The NGOs can play a useful role in disseminating such knowledge.

49. The majority (62.3 per cent) of the women labourers felt the need for government intervention to solve their problems. This shows that the majority of women labourers have faith in and expect the governmental machinery to solve their problems. Once they are aware of their rights and privileges they can solve their own problems. Most of the problems arise out of their illiteracy, ignorance and low income due to lack of skill. This low status of women can be removed by creating awareness about their rights and responsibilities and by empowering them in all respects.

50. The percentage of women labourers expecting benefits from NGOs is higher than those expecting benefits from GOs. Their expectations from the NGOs include regular employment chances, education facilities for their children, medical care free of cost, creating awareness about their rights, and, financial help. From the government side, they expect financial assistance, medical etc.

51. None of these 500 women labourers are members of any union. Two-thirds (66.4 per cent) of the women labourers expected such a union to help them to get higher wages from the employer, the help to get more benefits, to create awareness about good working environment. This shows that the majority of the women labourers are illiterates or have low level of education and they have also no skill and these drawbacks forced them into a low social and economic status. They have to be imparted sufficient knowledge about the importance of union/association. Therefore, unionisation among the rural labourers especially women labourers, is the need of the hour.

Suggestions for the Welfare of Women Labourers

1. Creation of more irrigation facilities is needed to increase employment opportunities in agriculture and allied activities.
2. To reduce the seasonal unemployment the Government's employment oriented programmes should be effectively implemented during the off-season. Thereby the landless labourers can be benefited.
3. Government and non-government agencies should organise literacy camps to create awareness about various employment programmes meant for landless labourers.
4. New employment avenues should be created based on needs and resources to reduce rural-rural and rural-urban migration.
5. To reduce the illiteracy level, adult education programmes should be effectively implemented for all rural women labourers.
6. The Government should provide adequate school facilities in the rural areas. It will improve the status of education in the villages.
7. To reduce the school dropouts at the primary level, the Government should provide high school facility in underdeveloped villages.
8. The government and non-government agencies should take necessary steps to organise entrepreneurial and skill development programmes for women labourers, to enhance their earning capacity.
9. Encouragement of non-farm activities in the study area will help the women labourers to get more employment chances in the non-farm sector as an alternative source of employment within their village area. Further, those labourers can use their unemployed days and enhance their earnings.
10. Rural housing programme should be implemented in the rural areas and the benefits should cover the poorest of the poor and the needy families.

11. Government should increase the access to institutional finance to landless labourers, particularly to women labourers.

12. Provision of institutional credit to the women labourers with easy access and without too many formalities will help to reduce the role of village moneylenders.

13. Starting of self-help groups in the rural areas will promote the saving habit among the women labourers and also it will strengthen their economic independence. Further, it will promote leadership qualities and ability to make decisions on their own.

14. Government should strictly insist on the employers providing minimum facilities like day care centre, first aid facility, canteen, toilet, rest room and creche in the workspot.

15. Steps should be taken to enforce the Minimum Wages Act and equal remuneration to equal work in the rural areas.

16. The government and non-government organisations may organise legal literacy campaigns to enable the rural women labourers to understand the various provisions relating to their occupation and to make proper use of them.

17. The government and non-government agencies should organise programmes to create awareness about the evil effect of alcoholism and smoking. Further, efforts should be taken to change the behaviours of women labourers' husbands to avoid unhealthy habits and retain their earnings for the welfare of their own families.

18. The women labourers should be given equal chance in the family rights and responsibilities. For this, proper awareness can be created among the women labourers' husbands. Also counselling programmes are needed to change the behaviour of the husbands and make them realise the importance of better environment in their family.

19. The government should take necessary step to increase the number of day care centres in the rural areas to look after the women labourers' children.

20. In order to protect the women labourers' rights and to ensure their due in all aspects, it is the need of the hour to organise the unorganised women labourers. Further, if they are able organise a union/association exclusively for women labourers, it will promote their social and economic status in the society.

21. The government and non-government agencies should take necessary efforts to make the women labourers aware of the various women development programmes through special awareness camps in rural areas. The NGOs can play a useful role in disseminating such knowledge.

22. The low status of women can be rectified by creating awareness about their rights and responsibilities and by empowering them in all respects. This awareness can solve most of their problems arising out of their illiteracy, ignorance and low income due to lack of skill.

23. The NGOs can play a useful role in making the labourers aware of their rights and responsibilities.

24. There is an urgent need to organise the women labourers to fight against their problems and so collective action is necessary in the form of union/ association to create awareness about their rights and privileges.

25. The women workers were found to suffer from different types of diseases and discomforts, and also there is dearth of medical facility in rural areas. They should have easy accessibility to medical attention and care workers should be encouraged to take advantage of medical relief and accident benefit scheme.

Suggestions for Further Research

The present study was confined to the problems of rural landless women labourers in Dindigul District. Similar studies may be conducted in other parts of Tamil Nadu at the state level and also at the national level. The present study can provide the basic framework for further researches in the related topics listed hereunder.

- Varied possibilities of employment opportunities for landless labourers may be explored.
- Another area which needs to be researched is to explore the strategies to involve the rural women in the development process.
- All the problems encountered by landless women labourers are due to lack of awareness, low education and low skill. This calls for involvement of non-government agencies in solving the problems of rural women labourers. Evolving a viable strategy for such intervention is yet another area for research.
- Health status and landless women labourers in rural areas.
- The possibility of organising self- help groups among women labourers.
- In order to tackle women's labour problems, the unorganised women labourers should be organised. To organise these unorganised labourers there is a need to evolve an appropriate strategy. This is yet another potential area for further research.

Conclusion

Despite more than five decades of interventions to raise the status of women since Independence, women in rural areas continue to be overwhelmed by economic and social barriers. Rural women throughout India, irrespective of caste or religion, continue to have a subordinate status both within the home and outside. Extent of awareness and access to education are prime determinants of rural women's status and role in the process of development. Limited awareness not only restricts economic options but affects their physical and social wellbeing. Lack of education and skill constrains rural women to work in spheres characterized by low skills and low pay. Women in rural areas have no access to formal credit, particularly because of their inability to provide guarantee in the form of assets. Moneylenders charge high interest rates and use unfair means like emotional and physical harassment to ensure repayment.

All the schemes launched by the government could not improve the living conditions and solve the problems of rural women's employment to the desired extent. Economic independence for rural women is the foundation of their rights, freedom and dignity. But the employment status of women in rural areas is far lower than that of men and the majority of women work in the unorganised sector. It is true that illiteracy and poverty marginalise the participation of women in gainful employment. The key to better employment is the participation of women in gainful employment. Education of women and diversification of employment opportunities supported by government projects promote women's employment. Women should be acquainted with the required skills and equip themselves with training in new trades for gainful employment. The easy accessibility of loans for self-employment has helped many women in improving their family income and gaining respect in the families.

In spite of constitutional safeguards, legislative measures, package of programmes by the government, no significant development has taken place in the socio-economic situation of women and they are still lagging behind men in their participation in the process of development. The Government has to make effective plans and policies and to take up concrete action for the employment of rural women. The most potentially effective way of empowering women is to enable and encourage their participation in workers' organizations. For this purpose, the administrative machinery should be made more vigilant towards the security of employed women in rural areas. Their involvement should increase in different activities that are taking place in the rural areas in which they are generally ignored. Further, the voluntary organisations should play an important role in implementing government programmes for the promotion of employment opportunities. The Government, along with the help of women groups and NGO's should establish vocational training and income generation centres.

The non-performance of the rural development process is due to poor awareness amongst the targeted populace about the schemes being launched for them. It has been found that the awareness level in the rural areas is very low. It is necessary to increase awareness among the women labourers regarding available opportunities, their rights and responsibilities through education from grassroots level in rural areas.

Appendix-A(2)

Gandhigram Rurual Insitute-Deemed University

TOPIC: " Problems of Landless Rural Women labourers in Dindigul District".

Interview schedule

Schedule No:

Name of the village :

Name of the block :

I. Personal Data :

1. Name of the Respondent :

2. Age :

3. Marital status : a) Married

   b) Un married

   c) Widow

   d) Seperated

   e) Destitute

4. Education : 1) Illiterate

   2) Literate

   3) Primary

   4) Secondary

5) Any other (specify)

5. Occupation : a) Main

b) Subsidiary

6. Religion : a) Hindu

b) Christian

c) Muslim

7. Caste :

8. Social class : FC/BC/MBC/DNC/OC/SC/ST

9. Family type : a) Nuclear

b) Joint

II. Family Data :

S. No.	*Member*	*Relation to the Respondents*	*Age*	*Sex*	*Education*	*Occupation*	*Monthly Income*

III. Housing condition

a) Ownership : Own leased Rented Construct (GO/NGO)

b) Structure : Hut Kutcha Pucca Mixed

c) Roof : Thatched Tiled Terraced

d) Condition : Good Moderate dilappidated.

IV. Asset position

S. No.	Item	Unit	Values in (Rs.)
1.	House		
2.	Plough/Agri-implements		
3.	Bullocks/Bullock cart		
4.	Milch animals		
5.	Goat and Sheep		
6.	Cycles/Moped		
7.	Utensil		
8.	Jewells		
9.	Savings		
10	Others specify		
	Total		

V. Monetary debt: (in Rs.)

S. No.	Source	Amo unt	Pur-pose	Repay ment	Balance
1.	Bank				
2.	Co-operative societies				
3.	Money lender				
4.	Relatives				
5.	Friends				
6.	Others (specify)				
	Total				

VI. Employment Position:

S.No	Member of Family	Employment in Days				Total No. of Unemployed Days
		Agriculture		Non-Agriculture		
		Main	Sub-sidary	Main	Sub-sidary	

VII. Annual Family Income:

S. No.	Earning Members in Family	Income from Agricultural		Income from Non-Agricultural		Total Income
		Main	Sub-sidary	Main	Sub-sidary	
1	Share of the Respondents income to the family income					
2.	Others					
	Total					

VIII. Family Expenditure

S.NO	Items	Expenditure incurred per month (in R.s)
1.	Food	
2.	House maintenance	
3.	Medical	
4.	Education	
5.	Food	
6.	Dress/Cosmetics	
7.	Electricity	
8.	Fuel/Fire wood/Electricity	
9.	Dress/Cosmetics	
10.	Festivals	
11.	Any other (specify)	

IX.Nature and Types of Employment

1. Nature of work : Daily/Contract Basis

2. Type of Work :

3 Reasons for Choosing : 1.

2.

3.

4.

4. What type of skill you have for
this employment : Yes No

5. Mentinon the advantage of special Skill(s)
needed for : 1.
this employment 2.

6. Source of your Employment : 1. Relative
2. Co-workers
3. Neighbours
4. Contractors
5. Farm Workers
6. Others(Specify)

7. Regular Employment days : Per Month

8. Reasons for Regular Employment :
1. 2. 3. 4.

9. No. of Unemployed days : Per Month

10. Reasons for Unemployment :
1. 2. 3. 4.

11. Problems in obtaining Employment : Yes No

12. List out the Problems in obtaining employment :
1. 2. 3. 4.

13. Did you met with any accident : Yes No

14. If yes, Did you get accedental benefits :
1. 2.

Wage and Working House

1. Wage per day : Male Female

2. Reasons for difference in wage : 1.

2.

3.

3. Wage in the form of : Cash Kind Both

4. Nature of wage payment : Daily/Weekly/Bimonthly/Monthly

5. Wage during sick/leave : Yes No

6. Awarness about the Minimum Wage Act : Yes No

7. Wage Distributor : Employer Agent Contracter

8. Exploitation in distribution of wage : Yes No

9. Types of Exploitation : 1.

2.

3.

4.

10. State the problem in getting wage : 1.

2.

3.

4.

11. Awareness about the minimum working hours : Yes No

12. Average Working Hours :

From _______AM to_______PM Perday

13. Number of days worked more than specified working hours:

_____________ Per Month

14. Wage for extra work : Rs___________ Per day or any other incentives 1.

2.

3.

4.

17. Work in the night hours : Yes No

18. Duration of work in the night hours :

From________Pm to _________Am

19. Special incentive for night work : Yes No

20. Type of incentive for night work : 1.

2.

3.

4.

21. Problems (If any) in the night work : 1.

2.

3.

4.

22. Family members allow for night work : Yes No

XI. Place(s) of Work

1. Work with in the village : Yes No

2. Work outside the village : Yes No

3. Types of work with in the village : 1.

2.

3.

4. Types of work outside the village : 1.

2.

3.

5. Mode of Reaching the workspot / home :

    1. Walk
    2. Cycle
    3. Public Transport
    4. Emphyer's transport
    5. Any other (specify)

6. People accompany with you in reaching the workspot :

    1. Husband
    2. Brother/sister/inlaws
    3. Co-workers
    4. Friends
    5. Anyother (specify)

7. What type of facilities available in the work spot?

1. Creche	: Yes No
2. Balwadi	: Yes No
3. Toilet	: Yes No
4. Canteen	: Yes No
5. Rest room	: Yes No
6. First Aid (medical)	: Yes No

8. Arrangement made by the employer :

    1.
    2.
    3.
    4.

Problems by the Employer, Co-workers and Contractor

Sl.	*Item*	*Employer*		*Co-worker*		*Contractor*	
		M	*F*	*M*	*F*	*M*	*F*
1.	Treatment Cordial Strain						
2.	Problem (if any) 1. 2. 3.						
3.	Reasons (s) 1. 2.						
4.	Solution(s) 1. 2. 3.						

XII. Problems with Husband

1. Husband's Age :

2. Occupation : Main: Subsidiary :

3. Earning : Rs. Perday

4. Employment days : Permonth

5. Unemployed days : Permonth

6. Accept your present employment : Yes No

7. Reasons for accepting employment :

   1.
   2.
   3.
   4.

8. Husband satisfied with your working times : Yes No

9. Reasons satisfied dissatisfied with working timings:

   1.
   2.
   3.
   4.

10. Getting support from :

    Obtaining employment

    Taking care of the children

    Sharing thefamily expenditure

    Tacking to workspot.

    Carryout household work/ activity

    Anyother

11. Whether husband brings the entire wage to home : Yes No

12. Reasons for not bringing the entire wage to home :

    1.

    2.

    3.

    4.

13. Husband satisfied with your present wage : Yes No

14. Reasons for husband's dissatisfaction towards your wage :

    1.

    2.

    3.

    4.

15. Husband and yourself work together in the same work spot :

    Yes No

16. Husband can share with your work : Yes No

17. The areas in which he can share the work :

    1.

    2.

    3.

    4.

18. Opinion about the husband : Asset Liabilities

19. Relationship with husband : Cordial Strain

20. General problems with husband : 1.

    2.

    3.

    4.

21. Suggested methods to solve the problems from husband :

1.

2.

3.

4.

22. Your employment create any misunderstanding with husband :

Yes No

23. Causes for misunderstanding : 1.

2.

3.

4.

24. Whether husband consult with you for decision making :

Yes No

25. Reasons for not consultation : 1.

2.

3.

4.

26. Husband's help during illness : Yes No

27. Areas of help during illness : 1.

2.

3.

4.

28. Reasons for not helping during illness :

1.

2.

3.

4.

29. Husband's treatment, when you did not go for work :

1. Cordial

2. Frustrated

3. Angry Habit Amount spend

30. Lists out the bad habits of your husband and amount spending :

1.

2.

3.

4.

Xiii The Children

1. Details regarding Children

S. No.	*Name of the Children*	*Attending schools and class*	*Getting scholarships / grant*	*Drop out and class*
1.				
2.				
3.				
4.				
5.				
6.				

2. Reasons for not attending school :

1.

2.

3.

3. Who takes care of your child when you go for work :

1. Father in-law

2. Mother in-law

3. Husband

4. Sister-in-law

5. Own son / daughter

6. Others (specify)

4. Problems related children's Education:

1.

2.

3.

5. Do you used to carry the children to the work-spot : Yes No

6. Facilities available in the wor-spot for children : Yes No

7. Specify the problems relating to the children : Male Female

8. Suggested remedial measures for solving problems of children :

Male Female

Xiv. Problem with Family Membersi. in Laws.

1. Inlaws encourage to go for work : Yes No

2. Reasons for encouragement/discouragement :

1.

2.

3.

3. Get support from inlaws for carryout :

1. House maintenance

2. Child rearing

3. Kitchen work

4. Washing

5. Collecting waterandfirewood

6. Tenting animals

7. Any other specify

4. Get recognition while taking important decisions : Yes No

5. Reasons for neglect : 1.

2.

3.

4.

6. Relationship with sister-in-law :

Cordial Strained Not Cordian Not Strained

Relationship with brother-in-law :

Cordial Strained Not Cordian Not Strained

Relationship with father-in-law :

Cordial Strained Not Cordian Not Strained

Relationship with mother-in-law :

Cordial Strained Not Cordian Not Strained

XV. Government and Non-government Measures to Solve the Problems of Women Labourers

1. Need Govt. intervention to solve the women labour problems :

Yes No

2. Awareness about the various programme

IRDP : Yes No

DWCRA : Yes No

JRY : Yes No

Any Other : Yes No

3. Sources of getting awareness : 1.

2.

3.

4. Opinion about NGO's for your development :

1. Employment
2. Education of children
3. Rights and powers
4. Medical
5. Other (specify)

6. Future suggestions :

Insurance :

Finance :

Medical benefit :

Accident benefit :

Employees Associations/Union

1. Member of any Union /Association : Yes No

2. Reason for joining / not : 1.

2.

3.

4.

3. Helpfulness of union/association to workers : 1.

4. Reasercher's Remarks : 1.

2.

3.

Appendix 'B'

Gandhigram Rural Institute
Department of Applied Research

Topic: "Problems of Rural Landless women Labourers in Dindigul District".

Format for Field Observation

1. Village:

2. Name of the respondent:

3. Occupation:

    1. Farm labourer 2. Non-farm worker labourer

4. Nature of work:

5. Work spot:

    Location of the work spot:

        1. Within the village.

        2. Out side the village

6. Points to be observed:

    1. Working conditions

    2. Facilities available at the work spot

    3. Housing conditions

Appendix 'C'

Gandhigram Rural Institute
Department of Applied Research

Topic: "Problems of Rural Landless women Labourers in Dindigul District".

Format for Focussed Group Discussion

1.Venue: Date: Time:

2. Members present:

1.	2.
3.	4.
5.	6.
7.	8.
9.	10.

3. Moderator:

4. Flow of Topic Guide for Discussion:

   1. General problems
   2. Gender discrimination
   3. Working conditions
   4. Facilities at work spot
   5. Wage difference among labourers
   6. Health problems and medical care

5. View points of the participants:

6. Suggestions and recommendations:

Bibliography

Books

Agarwal.A.N., *Agricultural Problems of India,* New Delhi: Vikas Publication (P) Ltd.,1996, pp. 1-15.

Brahmananda, *Dimensions of Rural Development in India,* New Delhi: Himalaya Publishing House, 1987, pp. 72-187.

Harbans Singh Sidhu, *Agricultural Development and Rural Labour,* New Delhi: Concept Publishing Company, 1991, pp. 102-257.

Immanuel, M., *Women and Development,* Ahmedabad: Karnavati Publications, 1998, pp. 21-98.

Kohli.A., *The State and Poverty in India:The Politics of Reform,* Cambridge: Cambridge University Press, (1987).

Laxmi Devi (ed), *Rural Psoverty and Unemployment,* New Delhi: Anmol Publication (P) Ltd , 1997, pp. 101-161.

Leela Gulathi, Agricultural labourers, Joyoce Lebra (ed), in *Women and Work in India - Continuity and change,* New Delhi: Promilla and Company, 1984, pp. 62-75.

Loes Schenk and Sandbersen, *Women and Seasonal Labour Migration,* New Delhi: Sage Publications, 1995, pp 23-155.

Radhakrishna, R. and Alakh, N. Sharma (eds), *Empowering Rural Labour in India,* New Delhi: Institute for Human Development, 1998, pp. 1-52.

Raj Mohini Sethi, *Women in Agriculture,* Jaipur: Rawat Publication, 1991, pp. 1-17.

Saran, A.B. and Sandhwar, A.N., *Problems of Women Workers in Unorganised Sectors,* New Delhi: Northern Book Centre, 1990, pp. 55-184.

Satya Sundaram, *Rural Development,* New Delhi: Himalaya Publishing House, 1997, pp. 208-217.

Savitha S.Joshi, *Women Workers at the Grossroot Level :A Sociological Study,* New Delhi: Ashish Publishing House, 1995, pp. 1-51.

The New Encyclopaedia Britanica, London: William Benton, 1979, pp. 25-26.

Tripathy, S.N., *Unorganised Women Labour in India,* New Delhi: Discovery Publishing House, 1996, pp. 1-123.

Uma Devi, Women As Agricultural Workers, *Women's Development, Problems and Prospects,* New Delhi: APH Publishing House, 1993, pp. 27-34.

Journals

Aditya Nigam, Rethinking the Unorganised Sector, *Social Action,* Vol. 47, April - June, 1997, pp. 125-130.

Giankaur, Female employment and wages in agriculture activities - Evidence from Rural Punjab, *Indian Journal of Agricultural Economics,* July -1994, Vol. XVI, No.3, pp. 54.

Lyakat Ali, Unorganised Labour and the Legislative Measures for their Welfare, *Social Action,* Vol. 47, April-June, pp. 182.

Martin Patrick, Discrimination, Time Allocation and Migration:A study of Unorganised Women, *The Indian Journal of Labour Economics,* Vol. 41, No. 3 (July-Sep. 1996) pp. 555-564.

Mishra, L., Organising the Unorganised Labour:Myth, Reality and Possibility, *The Indian Journal of Labour Economics,* Vol.41, No.1. Jan - Mar, 1998, pp. 55 - 66.

Nirmala et.al. (1998) Genderwise Minimum wages, Wage differentials and determinants: A micro analysis of

Agricultural labourers, *The Indian Journal of Labour Economics*, Vol.41, No. 2,1998.

Preet Rustogi, Women Employment in the Unorganised Sector: *Social Action*, Vol.47, April - June, pp. 167-179.

Ramesh, C. Shrivasthava, Ensuring Gender Equity and Equality, *Social Welfare*, July, 2000, pp. 33-36.

Renana Jhabvala, Minimum Wages Based on Worker's Needs, *Economic and Political Weekly*, March 7,1998, pp. 500-503.

Sharma, O.P., Unorganised Labour : Some Major Policy Issues, *Social Action*, Vol. 47, April to June, pp. 157-158.

Subesh K.Das, Fixation and Enforcement of minimum wages, *The Indian Journal of Labour Economics*, Vol. 41, No. 1, Apr-June 1998, pp 327-338.

Sucha Singh Gill, Migration of labour in India, *The Indian Journal of Labour Economics*, Vol. 41, No. 4, Oct to Dec, 1998, pp. 617-624.

Sukhadeo Thorat, Social Security in Unorganised Sector in India:How secure are the Seheduled Castes?, *The Indian Journal of Labour Economics*, Vol. 42, No. 3, 1999, pp. 454-466.

Reports

GOI (1992), Eight Five Year Plan, (1992-1995), Government of India, *Planning Commission*, New Delhi.

GOI(1987), Encyclopaedia of Social Work, *Ministry of Welfare*, Vol. 3, pp. 328.

GOI(1949), Report of the Committee on Fair Wages, Government of India, *Ministry of Labour*, New Delhi.

GOI(1991), Report of the National Commission on Wage Policy, Government of India, *Ministry of Labour*, New Delhi.

Watanable, S.H.(1976), "Minimum Wages in Developing Countries:Myth and Reality", *International Labour Review*,

Vol. 113, No. 3, May-June, pp. 343-58.

World Bank (1995) *World Development Report*, Workers in an Integrated World, New York, 1995.

GOI (1991), Dindigul-Anna District, 1991 Census, *Directorate of Census Operations*, Tamil Nadu, Government Central Press, Chennai, pp. 1-15.

NIRD (1999), *Rural Development Report*, p. 89.

Index

B

C

Q

R